WELL-CHOSEN WORDS

WELL-CHOSEN WORDS

Narrative Assessments and Report Card Comments

BRENDA MILLER POWER
KELLY CHANDLER

STENHOUSE PUBLISHERS
PORTLAND, MAINE

Stenhouse Publishers
www.stenhouse.com

Library of Congress Cataloging-in-Publication Data

Power, Brenda Miller.
   Well-chosen words : narrative assessments and report card comments
/ Brenda Miller Power, Kelly Chandler.
      p.   cm.
   Includes bibliographical references (p.   ).
   ISBN 1-57110-080-6
   1. Report cards—United States. 2. Students—Rating of—United
States. 3. Narration (Rhetoric) I. Chandler, Kelly, 1970–   .
II. Title.
LB2845.7.P69   1998
371.27′2—dc21   97-45939
                                                         CIP

Interior design by Catherine Hawkes
Cover photography by Andrew Edgar
Typeset by Technologies 'N Typography

Manufactured in the United States of America on acid-free paper
03 02 01 9 8 7 6 5 4 3 2

For Dolores Miller and Gail Gibson,
fine teachers and finer moms

Contents

THE NAKED TRUTH ABOUT WRITING ASSESSMENTS

*I would rather dance stark
naked in the teacher's lounge
than write.*

Diane Smith,
Kindergarten Teacher

What is it about writing that spooks so many teachers? What is it about assessing students that leaves so many of us feeling more inadequate than we do in any other realm of our teaching? Diane said these words at the start of a staff meeting devoted to developing skills in observing and writing about students. We believe she speaks for many teachers in expressing how daunting it can be to write assessments of learners.

Writing assessments of students is a serious test of your confidence as a writer—you are, after all, standing in judgment of your students even as you question whether you've placed your commas in the right place or split an infinitive. No wonder so many narrative assessments sound as if they were written by the unseen adult moaning in the background of the Charlie Brown cartoons—distant, indistinct, and irrelevant. Teachers rarely give themselves permission to write with humor, compassion, and enthusiasm in assessing students, even if these are the essential qualities in their relationships with learners.

Perhaps teachers are intimidated because we know that we can never do justice to our students' growth in a few paragraphs, let alone the two-inch comment section of the report card. There is no way to document fully what each student learns in our classrooms, and to bring that dynamic learning fully to life in a written assessment. And yet nothing is more rewarding than seeing a first grader's eyes light up at the moment she realizes the connection between those black squiggles on the page and the sounds of words. If you don't write it down and share it with others, who will? Nothing is more empowering than watching a parent's face as you explain in detail a milestone event in a child's learning, and you see the shift in the parent's body posture that signals a new respect for you as the professional charged with caring for that child daily. If you haven't accurately noted those moments in your students' learning, how will you be able to express them articulately?

A narrative is a way to help you to communicate these moments. If you have fears like Diane, this handbook can serve as a starting point for gaining confidence in writing and assessing students through narratives. If you've conquered your fears and write narrative assessments already, we hope to help you improve these narratives and lessen the time you spend doing it.

Because of the growth of student-centered instruction and the drive for alternative assessment of students, we believe all teachers will soon be required to write narrative assessments of students in some form. We don't know if "soon" means a few months or a decade, and we don't know if "some form" of narratives in your school will be a one-paragraph addendum to each report card or a three-page, single-spaced discussion of each student in your class.

There is no question, however, that the pressure increases every year for teachers to write about each student's strengths and needs, rather than just slotting codes into a report card. The pressure is explicit from national professional groups, which have published new standards in each discipline requiring individualized evaluation of students, and implicit within school districts, which have revised report cards containing bigger blank sections for comments by teachers.

This handbook is designed around a series of practical activities and advice to help you organize your materials, time, and vision for writing narrative assessments. Every teacher who reads this handbook will have a different goal. You may want to extend what you write about each student in the comment section of the report card by just a few sentences. Or you may already write extensively about each student in your assessments but want to improve the quality of your writing or cut the time needed to complete these narratives.

WHY WRITTEN ASSESSMENTS ARE ESSENTIAL

Some people still believe learning can be neatly packaged. They say those of us who disagree need to be more organized and linear (as well as discreet in criticizing skills and drills packages), and then we would see why traditional progressions on the report card make sense.

Life would be so much easier for teachers if learning did happen in a discrete, organized, linear fashion. But anyone who has looked closely at the diversity of learners in any first- or tenth-grade classroom knows that learning isn't always lockstep and systematic. For many students learning takes place, and natural progressions exist—they just can't be expressed easily through the comment codes on report cards. As Susan Ohanian notes:

> Learning is not something that takes place in finite steps at finite times . . . [I] suggest turning the table on any adults who profess a belief in mastery and asking them to list exactly what skills they have mastered. If you are feeling really devious you could give them a test on apostrophes, dividing fractions, or listing the planets in order of their distance from the sun. (p. 99)

What report cards and checklists often can do is highlight the specific content a student has mastered. This is frequently the least important component of a student's mastery of learning *how* to learn, and how to work in a community of learners. Narratives get you into that messy, complex realm of showing students' unique learning processes, their needs as learners, and how your role as a teacher varies according to those needs.

Most important, narratives endure. We both work with preservice teachers, and one of the activities we have them do is to write a learning history describing themselves at different ages in school. Many of our students eagerly go through attics and drawers at home, looking for report cards from their childhood. Inevitably, when they find the cards they are disappointed. The A's and B's, Satisfactories and Unsatisfactories, give them little or no sense of what they were like as a learner in first or fifth or eleventh grade. Even the briefest of comments on any report card provide them with the only understanding of who they were in the class and how the teacher saw them.

Remember as you begin this process that you are writing words that have the potential to live well beyond your time with students. These words will be remembered, saved, and sometimes cherished. If you invest a lot in your teaching, you owe it to yourself and your students to include some written narratives in your assessment scheme.

After all, parents and students aren't the only ones who benefit from narrative assessments. We believe that teachers do, too. We learned to write narratives from our work in public schools. We continue to write them for our university students now, even though we're not required to do so. Although this process takes a good deal of energy and time, the payoff is worth it. We've found that crafting narratives helps us to reflect on our teaching, take stock of every learner's growth, and consider next steps for each of those learners. We hope that writing narratives will serve the same purposes for you.

GETTING STARTED

The starting point for any teacher reading this handbook is to realize you are already a skilled evaluator of your students and their needs.

Thoughtful teachers are constantly assessing each student's growth, and what they have to do next to help that learner. Fine teachers notice individual students while simultaneously thinking about what the whole class might need next. It's a dynamic process—sometimes invigorating, sometimes exhausting. Many good teachers joke about the difference between the notes in their planbook and what really happens every day in the classroom. This gap exists because teachers make adjustments in the middle of the day as they observe their students and use what they see to inform their instruction. Learning to write good assessments of students is realizing what skills you have in observing and writing about students, and then developing those skills into strengths.

We've organized this handbook around a series of exercises that will help you think about ways to expand or improve your narrative assessments of students. We know every teacher is different. The elementary teacher who has 25 students in her class has far different needs than the tenth-grade teacher who strives to keep track of 156 students each day. Specialists must balance their personal goals for narrative assessments with the legal and district requirements regarding documentation. Adapt our principles to your needs and those of your students.

We urge you, regardless of your goals, to find a colleague who is willing to work with you to meet them. Many of the extensions work best when they are discussed with a peer. Your partner in revising your assessment scheme needn't teach at the same grade level; she might even work at a different school. But you'll move more quickly toward your goal if you have someone to discuss the pitfalls and roadblocks with along the way.

EXTENSIONS

1. Try to find at least one friend or colleague willing to do the activities in this handbook with you.

It's possible to do the activities in this handbook on your own—many teachers have done so and learned a lot from them. But a partner or team from your school can really help you over the rough spots in learning to write assessments. You're going to need some support if you want to make substantial changes in the way you write assessments of students, and it's best to identify someone who might help at the start.

Once you find a colleague who is willing to try the activities in this handbook with you, set aside some time each week to meet or talk together. It might be during a regular planning period you share, or before or after school one day per week. The difference between success and failure in making changes usually comes down to who has support at the start of the change process.

2. Set some goals for improving your written narratives.
If your district is mandating more written assessment of students, these goals might be mandated for you. But if you have some choice in the matter, you'll want to think about what goals are reasonable and realistic for you. For some teachers, extending comments by a sentence or two on report cards would be a realistic goal. Others might want to be more specific in the comments they write about students, or develop more focused and concrete recommendations in their assessment narratives.

You may want to start by thinking about what you do well in assessing students. Are you well organized in your work? Do you take particular care with the special needs students in your classroom? Do you already keep some kind of anecdotal records?

WRITE THREE STRENGTHS YOU HAVE IN EVALUATING STUDENTS:

1. _____

2. _____

3. _____

Now think about what you want to do better in writing assessments of students. Take a few moments to think about and jot down your goals for improving your assessments:

MY GOALS:

1. _____

2. _____

3. _____

If you have a friend or colleague who is using this handbook with you, spend some time the first week talking about your strengths and needs when it comes to assessing students. You may find that some of your needs match the strengths of your partner, and this can be a good starting point for finding ways to collaborate.

3. Write a one-paragraph assessment of someone you know well.
Choose someone you've known for a long time—a sibling, son or daughter, a mate—and write a one-paragraph assessment of him or her as a learner.

Make a list of what kinds of information you included. Why did you choose to include these things? What makes them important? How did you know what to write? What experiences led you to those conclusions about this learner? How can you, as a teacher, glean the same kinds of information about your students?

4. Think about a written assessment someone did of you that was meaningful.

Why was it important to you? In what form was the evaluation? When teachers we work with do this exercise, the assessments that are meaningful to them are often brief. What seems to matter most is that the assessment was specific and provided the response needed at that moment in time.

If you believe that narrative assessments are the right response at the right time for your students, you will need to make some decisions. You'll have to consider the audience for your narratives, and you'll have to determine how to fit writing them into your busy teaching schedule. We hope that the next chapter will help you to do both of these tasks.

2 START SMALL AND BUILD: SETTING LIMITS AND COMMUNICATING WITH PARENTS

E very teacher despises a cheater. We want students to do their own work, take pride in it, and stand on their personal accomplishments as learners. We expect the same of ourselves as teachers, and that independent and honest streak in fine teachers has led to many innovations in our profession. But it also gets in the way of teachers learning how to write narrative assessments of students.

We've titled this chapter "Start Small and Build," but it could just as easily be titled "Borrow, Steal, and Cut Corners." We don't think that this more realistic title would sit well with our honest, hardworking readers. Yet we've discovered that teachers who write quality assessments of students are living oxymorons—honest cheaters—as they learn how to budget time, resources, and energy in their evaluation scheme.

To get started, you need to realize it is *not* cheating to:

1. Write assessments of only one subject area if you are an elementary teacher.

You are responsible for your students' learning in all areas, but many times the best way to learn to write assessments is to focus on the curricular area you are most confident in (e.g., reading, science, math). Parents will learn about the other subjects through the codes already used in the report card, and you'll be starting from your strength.

2. Write assessments of only one class if you teach many different classes of adolescents.
If you work with 150 students a day, it's tough even to imagine how you'll find time to write a cogent paragraph or more about each student, especially when you're just beginning to build your narrative writing skills. So don't even try—pick one class that you will take care to assess in writing for the quarter. You can then use what you learn from the small group to move toward assessing all students as your end goal.

3. Write a section about class goals and activities for all students, with only a paragraph or two that is tailored to the individual needs and strengths of each student.
Many teachers write an introductory section in their narratives that is the same for all students, detailing the work of the class community over the quarter or year. This allows parents and other readers of the narrative to view the student's achievements within the context of the teacher's aims and purposes for the entire learning community. Teachers take great care to craft those opening paragraphs to represent the class well. We've seen overviews that range from a few sentences about the essential topics and skills covered in a unit to lengthy summaries of the activities completed during a term.

A team of teachers doing an integrated literacy theme with third, fourth, and fifth graders chose to write this introduction:

> Ancient Egypt has been the backdrop for this reading and writing adventure. Our community of eight- to ten-year-old "archaeologists" has learned how and why pharaohs were mummified, how and for what purpose the pyramids were built, some of the ancient Egyptians' beliefs, and how to dig like a master archaeologist. Our primary goal through all these

hands-on projects has been to promote a love of and enthusiasm for reading and writing, and to encourage children to see the connections between reading and writing. We have immersed the students in a wealth of print related to ancient Egypt, including nonfiction and fiction texts, poems, charts, posters, and daily letters. The children have been encouraged to read and interact with all of these inviting print resources within the room. We have used audiotapes and videotapes to meet the needs of other learning styles as well. Some of the vocabulary we have been using includes: archaeology, mummies, pyramids, sarcophagus, hieroglyphics, cartouch, papyrus, noves, and apprentice. Learning has taken place during this journey back in time, and each child has taken a piece of Egypt away with them.

The teachers then wrote individual comments about each child from their class, working within the context of the theme.

4. Write your assessments with a pen instead of typing them. Or type your assessments instead of handwriting them.

We have worked with teachers who get tripped up because of expectations of what the final product will look like. If you always work at the computer, you can cut and paste your comments into the comment section of the report card rather than writing them. If you like writing in bed with a cup of tea and a stack of student folders, don't feel you're shortchanging your students and parents because your comments are handwritten, not typed.

5. Mine a checklist.

We know some teachers who use checklists as the starting point for their written assessments. Instead of writing a paragraph that stands alone, they write detailed notes in the margins of the checklist (see Figure 2.1). For many teachers, this process is less intimidating than facing a blank page, yet it provides far more personalized and precise

Figure 2.1 Checklist with marginal comments

Literature Circle Participation Checklist

Isaac
Quarter 2

NA = not assessed; NY = not yet demonstrated; IP = in progress; CD = consistently demonstrated

PREPARATION

	NA	NY	IP	CD
1. Comes to meetings with assigned reading completed.			✓	
2. Comes to meetings with learning log entry prepared.			✓	

1. Enjoyed both Shiloh and Island of Blue Dolphins — frequently reads ahead of group.
2. (Need to be more consistent about stopping to respond/reflect before going on in reading)

GROUP PARTICIPATION

	NA	NY	IP	CD
1. Makes regular contributions to discussion.				✓
2. Considers other points of view.				✓
3. Listens actively and respectfully to others.				✓
4. Invites other members to participate.			✓	
5. Asks questions when s/he doesn't understand.			✓	

Almost always takes on role of leader (unofficial)

Especially when discussion involves an argument. Can hold his own & prove a point, but needs to see where his viewpoint is coming from.

4. i.e. to Andrea: "Did you have something to add?" I'm encouraging this.
5. Tends to ask me, not other group members.

READING SKILLS AND STRATEGIES

	NA	NY	IP	CD
1. Able to summarize or retell reading.				✓
2. Discusses author's purpose.			✓	
3. Makes predictions.				✓
4. Monitors comprehension.			✓	
5. Recognizes figurative language.		✓		

1. Sometimes has a tendency to tell too much
5. I'll be recommending some books to him that have clear examples of this. Verbally, not in log.

information than a code or a check in the appropriate box. If you are just beginning to write narratives, you might want to consider this option.

At Mapleton Elementary School, the staff has developed a developmental continuum for writers and readers based on information from several professional books. When parents receive narrative assessments, they also receive a copy of this checklist (see Figure 2.2), which is used by all K–5 teachers. Teachers' narratives (see Figure 2.3 for a sample) are meant to complement the checklist by providing examples of each child's learning in the areas it describes; neither tool is intended to stand alone. You could also develop a similar form for spelling development. Parents are often very concerned about their child's spelling, and a checklist or continuum might be a great tool for educating them.

Checklists can also help focus your notetaking and ensure that you gather information about each child in the areas that you or your district have identified as important. If you periodically take notes using the categories as a guide, you will have adequate data to place each learner on a developmental continuum. You will also be able to describe the ways in which that continuum might not fit the child's learning quirks. When it comes time to write an assessment, you'll have a wealth of information to draw on.

Now that we've given you permission to cut a few corners and lower your sights a bit, you'll need to formalize your starting point for writing assessments of students. Look back at the goals you set in Chapter 1. Consider your goals in light of more modest expectations. Is the best starting point for you to work with only one of your high school English classes, or to write assessments of your third graders in science this spring?

List your goals again, trying to narrow the scope of when and what you will write about here:

1. _____

2. _____

Before you begin collecting information for your narratives, you will need to consider where narratives fit on your palette of assessment

FIGURE 2.2   Developmental continuum used by Mapleton Elementary School

Three Stages of Reading Development

Emergent Readers

Children at this stage exhibit "reading-like" behavior as they read stories over and over. This is actually an approximation and retelling of the text as the reader relies on memory and experience with the story in order to read it. The children ask others to read their favorite stories and are aware when the reader leaves out part of the text. They are aware of print in their environment and read familiar signs. The emergent reader is developing an appetite and curiosity for understanding what print is all about. They are beginning to see that print, as well as illustrations, carry meaningful messages.

Early Readers

The early readers are moving from "reading-like" behavior to word-by-word reading. The readers may point with fingers as they read. They no longer memorize favorite stories, but try to match a printed word with a spoken word, and they expect the story to make sense. They choose to read independently and are very excited about their abilities to do so. The early readers begin to develop a variety of reading strategies—such as rereading when the text does not make sense, applying experiences of oral language to the text, and confirming predictions by checking visual clues.

Fluent Readers

The fluent readers are very interested in different kinds of text. They move into silent reading, and work on strategies until they have control over the reading process. Because of this, they read more difficult material and greater quantities of text. At this stage, the readers, in order to work with difficult text, may revert to word-by-word reading, characteristic of the early reader. The type of book choices these readers make reflect their level of experience with texts.

Three Stages of Writing Development

Emergent Writers

The emergent writers are those who are imitating writing. These are often children who have been read to and have had opportunities to interact with books. They have seen people read and write and have experimented with paper and writing tools. They are beginning to notice print in their environment, such as the McDonald's and Burger King signs, and they print on cereal boxes. The emergent writers may scribble, draw a picture, and write a few letters in their names. They can reread their own writing.

Early Writers

The early writers understand that speech can be written down. These writers are beginning to realize that conventions control writing and that writing can be reread. The children do quite a bit of erasing as they struggle with conventions, letter formation, and spelling. they reread to regain understanding lost during these spelling and penmanship struggles.

Fluent Writers

The fluent writers have gradually gained control over writing conventions and letter formations and are therefore writing with ease. They realize the many purposes of writing. They refine their writing to say what they mean and care about quality. The fluent writers initiate rewriting and revision. They take more time to complete their text and are conscious of how they "go about writing." They see that writing involves more than conventions and recognize the need for developing a theme in detail.

FIGURE 2.3 A narrative to accompany developmental continuum

> *Alexia is in the fluent stage of reading. She is able to use a variety of reading strategies flexibly. She often rereads when she gets confused, and I recently observed her scanning ahead to help her puzzle out a story that had difficult proper names. (When she looked ahead to see "polar bear," it helped her read "Mr. Adair" because she understood the rhyme quality of the book.) She reads orally with expression and enjoys and shares the humor she finds in books. She also contributes thoughtful and insightful comments when we are discussing authors, illustrators, and books.*

tools. Is the narrative a primary means of assessment or a supplement? If you are a novice at writing narrative assessments, we recommend presenting them to parents as a supplement at the start.

Knowing what is already being communicated with report cards will also help you identify what is important to include in your narrative and avoid duplicating information that appears in other assessments. For example, if your report card indicates whether or not a student is reading "at grade level," there is little need to discuss this in your narrative. If your school has adopted a checklist on spelling development, you may not need to write much about spelling.

We caution you against using narrative assessments to do work for you that other tools could or should do. In one high school, for example, teachers were wasting time and space by repeatedly listing missing assignments in their midterm progress reports. Claudia LaBrie, a high school social studies teacher, came up with a solution: she types out a master list of assignments for the term and photocopies it for each student. It takes only a minute to check off each completed assignment (something she often does with individual students), and she can use the bottom of the sheet for comments about growth she's noticed over the term (see Figure 2.4). Sometimes she uses a yellow highlighter to make missing work particularly evident.

Conversely, you may discover that certain aspects of students' learning (e.g., their ability to work in a group or their strategies for problem solving) never get discussed in any of your existing assessment forms. You may choose to highlight these in your narratives.

You'll also want to think about the best time to write narratives. If your parent conferences are scheduled in October or November and nearly all parents attend, it doesn't make sense to write detailed narratives at this point in the year when you will be in the midst of many time-consuming face-to-face meetings. (See Figure 3.2 for an example of a narrative report card that makes the reporting schedule clear for parents.) The end of the school year can also prove to be a difficult time for writing narratives, since this is the time when many teachers are thinking about their classes for the next fall or are busy determining placements and plans for students who haven't met academic goals during the year.

If you want to start small and build a narrative assessment program, you will find the winter months best for assessing and writing. Teachers know students well enough at this point to do some good writing, and there is still time to use what you've learned from the written assessments to make adjustments to your curriculum and plans for each student.

PARENTS AND ASSESSMENTS

Parents are usually the main recipients of our narrative assessments. It's important before you begin to write narrative assessments to remember that most parents experienced a different kind of reporting system than the one we're suggesting, as did most teachers. Rarely, if ever, were comments about performance more detailed than "Good student" or "Not working up to potential." Because of this, many

FIGURE 2.4   Claudia LaBrie's progress report

Ms.LaBrie   **Social Studies 9**   **Quarter 3**

Name __Mitch Higgins_____   Day _2_ Block _1_

Essential Question: What are my rights and responsibilities in my community?

I. CITIZENSHIP RESEARCH PAPER   40% (400 points)

2/9	Documentation of Research	_50_ of 50
2/13	Outline/Paragraph Sketch/Web	_50_ of 50
2/23	Rough Draft	_65_ of 75
2/25	Peer Edit	_72_ of 75
3/2	Final Draft	_140_ of 150

II. HISTORICAL FICTION NOVEL 30% (300 points)

3/6	Chapter Reflection 1	_55_ of 60
3/13	Chapter Reflection 2	_60_ of 60
3/20	Chapter Reflection 3	_55_ of 60
3/27	Booktalk	_110_ of 120

III. CLASS PARTICIPATION   15% (150 points)

_120_ of 150

IV. DAILY ASSIGNMENTS 15% (150 points)

3/9	Find lobbying or spec. interest group article in news	_25_ of 25
3/11	Find article about the president in news	_25_ of 25
3/16	Your interpretation of the first 10 Amendments	_20_ of 25
3/17	Groupwork on classroom Bill of Rights	_25_ of 25
3/24	Written response to the play "1776"	_23_ of 25
4/1	Find info on local, state, and national reps	_25_ of 25

TOTAL POINTS _920_ **of 1000**   **GRADE** _A⁻_

ATTENDANCE

Tardy Unexcused _1_ Tardy Excused _0_ Absent Unexcused _0_ Absent Excused _2_

Comments:

Mitch has been a leader in both whole-class and small
group discussions. Not only does he regularly offer
his opinions and back them up with evidence, but
he's also careful to solicit opinions from quieter
group members. He seemed to enjoy his book choice,
Legacy by James Michener.

parents are unsure of what an evaluation narrative should contain. Some of them may want it to serve as an expanded traditional report card, or "rank card," especially if the narrative is substituted for letter or number grades. For these parents, the best yardstick of achievement is one that lies across the heads of other students, an attitude that is reinforced by teachers' comments like "Jenny is among the best readers in her class" or "Although most of the children are beginning to write, Brad continues to draw during writing workshop."

Many teachers have moved away from comparing students in their teaching—ranking kids can foster competition and undermine collaborative efforts. We prefer to focus on the individual's growth over time, celebrating small steps and pointing to new challenges. We want our assessment tools to reflect this learner-centered philosophy.

While we respect the need for parents to know that their children are meeting grade level norms, it is possible to help them view their child's individual achievements and your expectations in a thoughtful way. In our experience, parents want more than anything else for their child to be known as an individual learner to the teacher. After receiving even a brief written narrative, parents rarely value the old system of reporting as much as the detailed, personalized information about their child found in a narrative.

If parents are the primary audience for your narratives, you need to write in a language that is accessible to them. Like any profession, education has a host of specialized vocabulary associated with it: guided reading, time on task, competencies, outcomes, running records, risk taking, collaborative learning, portfolio assessment, and so on. Because educators are familiar with these terms, we may not even realize that they can be confusing, off-putting, or incomprehensible to people who spend little time in schools. Our narratives need to be written in ways that invite parents into conversations with us, not ways that exclude them.

The more you know about your students' parents, the less you'll have to treat them like generic readers. You may feel more comfortable using certain terms (for example, "emergent reader" or "math manipulatives") if you explain them before you begin writing narratives.

If you've had telephone conversations with a parent about a particular concern, you may choose to emphasize it more in that student's narrative than you would in others. You may use different language when writing about a child whose parent is an elementary teacher at another school.

As long as you're not required to fit your narratives in a designated box on the report card, you may want to try formatting them as an informal letter. The letter form helps to reinforce one of the narrative's most important purposes—communication—and it seems more personal to parents. Some teachers find that addressing parents directly ("Dear Mr. and Mrs. Johnson") helps them to keep their audience squarely in mind as they write.

The start of building a manageable assessment system is always thinking about your audience, the limits of your time, and your purposes in writing evaluations. The following extensions will help you understand who your audience is and what boundaries you need to set for these assessments.

EXTENSIONS

1. Research parents' assessment needs.
Informally interview several friends (preferably not teachers) who are parents of school-age children. What kinds of information do they desire most from their child's teachers? Are they satisfied with the reporting that they currently receive? What suggestions for improved communication do they have? Compare your results with a colleague who has done the same thing.

2. Survey parents' assessment expectations.
Send home a survey (see Figure 2.5 for an example) to your students' parents about their experiences with assessment and their expectations for their child. You might also ask these questions during parent conferences.

FIGURE 2.5   A parent survey form

Parent Survey About Assessment and Evaluation

Parent Name _____
(optional)

Student Name _____
(optional)

1. What do you remember about report cards or other assessments from your own schooling?

2. What have your child's previous teachers done that was helpful in communicating your child's learning to you?

3. What kinds of information would you like conveyed in a narrative assessment about your child's learning?

4. Think of a "learning breakthrough" that happened with your child at home at any point. Explain the situation, and why you considered it a breakthrough.

3. State your assessment goals.

After you have determined your own small starting point for writing narrative assessments (either doing one curricular area if you are an elementary teacher, or only one class if you work at the middle or secondary level), write a letter to parents explaining your goals with your new assessment program. If you don't know where to begin, Figures 2.6 and 2.7 may help. Feel free to steal, borrow, or revise the parts that work for you.

FIGURE 2.6   A parent letter from an elementary teacher

Dear Parents:

This quarter I will be trying a new kind of assessment of your child. I will be writing a narrative that describes your child's learning in science. While the report card will still cover all curricular areas, science is a special focus this quarter for our class. We will be studying mammals, and my assessments will include interviewing students to discover what they know already about mammals, observing them work with their peers, and evaluating the reports they complete individually on a specific mammal.

The written evaluation of your child that you receive at the end of the quarter will include an introduction that describes the goals of the science program for all students, and the activities that took place throughout the quarter. I will also include a paragraph or two about what your child learned, his or her strengths as a learner, and areas of need we will work on together next quarter.

This new science assessment program is part of a year-long effort I've initiated to develop my skills in observing students and writing about their progress. In the past, many parents have been dissatisfied with the limited information the report card provides in describing their child's learning. I want to do a better job describing that learning to you, and this is my attempt to begin to write the more detailed descriptions many of you want. If you could spare a few moments, I would appreciate it if you would fill out the attached survey about your own experiences with assessment, and what you would like me to notice and tend to as I evaluate your child's learning.

If you have any questions about this new assessment program, please let me know. And if you have any special materials (books, stuffed animals) you would like to loan to our classroom library during the mammal unit, please send them along! I know the children will enjoy this unit, and I will enjoy watching them learn.

Sincerely,

FIGURE 2.7   A parent letter from a secondary teacher

Dear Parents:

The students have been working diligently on their speeches for the mock abolition meeting in two weeks. Most of them have done a lot of library research on the historical figures they will play, and they're beginning to draft their speeches. A few of them are even designing costumes for their characters and gathering some nineteenth-century props. You might want to ask your son or daughter where he or she is in this process.

Because this assignment is such a long-term one, requiring everyone to use reading, writing, researching, and speaking skills, I've decided to write brief narrative assessments of the students. A simple letter grade will not tell the story of students' growth or investment in this project. Nor will it be able to demonstrate how they've worked together as a class to make the meeting happen.

As a group, we've designed a scoring guide for the actual performance of the speech. The guide includes these three categories—Distinguished, Competent, and Unacceptable—and describes each of them. This way, the students know ahead of time what they need to do. Anyone who receives an "Unacceptable" will need to redo this assignment at a later date.

We'll be holding the mock meeting during third period (9:10–10:00) on Friday, January 24. Please join us if you can. During the week of January 27–31, students will be bringing home a letter from me that will describe students' performance on their speeches, as well as discuss their work on the project in general. Look for it, and give me a call at school if it doesn't arrive.

Thank you for supporting your child.

Sincerely,

3 BIG IDEAS IN LITTLE BOXES: REPORT CARD NARRATIVES

A favorite toy among children, the Russian nesting doll is a colorfully painted wooden figurine that unscrews at the waist to reveal an exact replica of itself, only smaller. The figurines get progressively tinier as they near the center, where there is a wee doll that cannot be opened.

We believe many books on writing narrative assessments start from the wrong place. They ask teachers to begin with that large, final figurine—a long, detailed narrative that perfectly captures the accomplishments and future directions of a learner—when they should ask teachers to start with the smallest doll. These expectations aren't realistic for many of us, and they don't fit the assessment demands in most schools now.

We want you to start with that tiny doll by crafting short, focused pieces that represent the students in your class and that can fit in a report card box. This is the task many teachers face every six to ten weeks when they fill out report cards and reach the comment section.

These two-inch spaces present two distinct challenges: how to keep brief narratives from sounding the same; and how to select a few sentences from the hundreds of things you could say about each child. But if they are done well, your narratives will be like the tiny figure at the heart of a nesting doll: the base model from which more extensive writing can be built.

You might be surprised at how easy it is to write distinctive comments about your students. With a bit of preparation, strategies for noticing all children, and some creative integration of your assessment writing into the curriculum, you will soon be filling those small report card comment boxes with lively, informative prose.

Preparing to Write

If your report card allows you to write only a few sentences about each student, a bit of advance planning is necessary if you want to be specific and concrete. It's essential that you begin at least two or three weeks before report cards are due. If you put in just a few hours in the weeks before the report comments are written, you will find you save yourself lots of stress the final days before report cards are due.

Begin by using a class list to help you think about each student before writing. Brainstorm two or three adjectives to describe each student as a learner in your class, challenging yourself to make them different for every student in the group. It doesn't take more than thirty minutes for most teachers to go through the class list, describing each student. A few students will remain enigmas to you, and you will need to pay special attention to them in the weeks before you fill out cards. Writing your assessments the day before they're due in your administrator's box may make it impossible to fill in the knowledge gaps for those students.

Then make brief notes during class time in the two or three weeks before you fill out report cards to support your choice of adjectives: an observation from workshop time, a specific piece of writing, a direct quote from a discussion (see Figure 3.1). We think it's much more effective to provide parents with one or two narrowly focused and relevant comments about their child than it is to make broad, generic statements.

You might also consider brainstorming a list of sentence "stems" that will help you generate meaningful narratives. For example, you might provide yourself with the following prompts if you're stumped for something to say about a child:

- ▾ Jessica's best work of the quarter was . . .

- ▾ Jonathan has shown improvement in . . .

- ▾ This term I was glad to see Erin . . .

- ▾ Ask Melissa to talk about . . .

- ▾ This term Connor challenged himself by . . .

Varying the stems you use may help you vary your narratives and remind you of the different options available to you—even in such a small space.

For some teachers freewriting provides a helpful beginning to their brief narratives. These quickly written, uncensored thoughts about a child often yield a kernel of an idea that is appropriate for the comment box. As you become more experienced at writing assessments, these freewrites may become the skeleton of a lengthy narrative, rather than just the source of a few sentences.

Missing Kids

No matter how diligent you are about anecdotal record keeping, there will always be some students who, for a variety of reasons, get left out of your notes. In his book, *A Fresh Look at Writing* (1994), Donald Graves suggests a written exercise in which teachers list from memory

FIGURE 3.1   Lois Pangburn's planning for narratives about her first graders

Student	Descriptors	Example	Report Card Narrative
Krista	caretaking, kind	Jeff's coming to class	Krista is such an important part of the class community. She is very sensitive to others' feelings. Recently, she helped a new student feel more comfortable with our routine.
Martin	knowledgeable, curious	nonfiction readalouds	Martin brings lots of prior knowledge about the natural world to our discussions. Recently, he shared the definition of "photosynthesis" with us during a readaloud.
Marcy	mischievous, playful	writing workshop	Marcy's mischievous sense of humor comes through in her writing. She likes to write puns and jokes in her journal, and her playful "Once upon a bird" beginning to a story has been borrowed by several other classmates.
Sarah	diligent, hardworking	independent reading	Sarah works hard at improving her independent reading skills. After practicing her books numerous times, she often seeks out adults to listen to her read aloud.
Angela	thoughtful, helpful	classroom transitions	Angela is always willing to help keep our classroom neat and orderly. She's also quick and thoughtful about assisting others with chores during pick-up time.
Johnny	creative, innovative	bird story in journal	Johnny recently wrote a wonderful piece in his journal called "The Never-Ending Bird Story." Twenty pages long (!), it was creative in its style and innovative in its illustrations.

all the names of the students in a particular class. He then instructs his reader to write in another column something about each student's interests and experiences. "Note which names you remember first," he writes. "I find that they are often the students I enjoy most and those about whom I worry the most. Some children I won't remember. The missing children are often those who don't stand out, who get lost, or who are noticed only after three days of absence" (p. 25).

As teachers, we tend to gather a lot of information about students at the extremes. If you despair about Jamie ever learning to read or you think Chris may become the next William Faulkner, those observations are probably in your notes. If Maggie is most likely to be found anywhere but in her seat, you've probably written about your frustration with her—or it's close to the front of your brain when you sit down to write her narrative.

The kids we tend to miss are often less distinct characters in our classroom casts. They mind their own business, do their homework, and recede into the background. In our experience, girls make up a large percentage of these students who are, to use Myra and David Sadker's (1994) phrase, "missing in interaction." Writing good narrative assessments depends on rich data about how students interact with their work, each other, and you. As one teacher told Kelly, "When you don't know much about a kid, it's a lot harder to fake it in a narrative than on a traditional report card."

In order not to miss certain students in your observations, you will need to build in times when you quickly scan your thoughts on each student. Review your notes on a regular basis—say, every other Thursday while your students are in gym, or while you're monitoring study hall—and note how much information you have for each student. Some teachers even like to use a class list to "tally" the pieces of data they've collected over the last few weeks. When you identify the three or four students about whom you know the least, you can focus on them in your notetaking over the next few days.

Since many of the students we "miss" in our notetaking tend to be reticent about speaking up during large-group discussions, make sure that some of your notetaking occurs in situations when they will feel more comfortable participating. Observe their participation in small groups, their behavior during independent work time, and make sure to schedule individual conferences frequently with those students.

Building Habits and Routines

Once you've carved out some time to observe, write, and comment on the work of all your students, there are a few additional strategies to use that will help you write meaningful comments for students and parents.

First, focus on the positive. Students who struggle with course work or exasperate you will have those needs revealed by other notations on the report card (i. e., a letter grade or a code for behavior). Many negative adjectives can be reworked to suggest strengths. "Restless" and "easily distracted" students can often be characterized as "very energetic." If you focus on what students can do well in the written comments, you and parents can build from these strengths. Students and parents are usually painfully aware of what isn't going well, and negative comments can be the start of breakdowns in communication. Regardless of how frustrating a student is, a narrative is not a disciplinary referral nor the place to catalogue that student's sins. Better to open the door to more dialogue with the parents of challenging students by showing you do appreciate their strengths and talents as learners in the brief comment space.

Second, learn to ask for help from colleagues. We work too much in isolation in schools, and nothing is more solitary and oppressive than that stressful feeling of everyone scribbling away frantically the day before report cards are due, alone in their classrooms. Once you've brainstormed adjectives and incidents, you may want to elicit the support of colleagues in describing your students. Art, music, and physical education teachers have often observed your students for years, not months. You know these colleagues best—one of them might be willing to observe a couple of your students during their class to provide more material for fleshing out your narratives. Instructional aides and student interns may also be able to provide you with valuable observations about the students with whom they have worked.

Third, write the easy comments first. You will build your skills in writing assessments if you start with the students who are easy to describe. You probably can think of an incident or two for at least a small number of your students that would be appropriate for the report card box. Write these first, saving the most challenging comments for last. As your confidence in writing specific comments grows, you will find you have more to say about these enigmatic students than you realized.

Once you've begun the process of writing specific comments, it's very helpful to look at what you've written about a student during the previous term or terms—both to avoid duplication and as a potential source of inspiration. If information is available from previous years, consider those comments. You may want to start a folder with your lists of adjectives, comment brainstorms, and drafts from past quarters. What strengths were mentioned previously? How have these developed or changed? What didn't you have space to mention last term that you could include this term? You might also want to look at any recommendations you wrote in the past, in order to provide an update on students' progress.

Finally, try always to tie your recommendations to classroom-based information. One of the most important goals of the comment section should be to strengthen links between home and school. You can do this most effectively by pairing recommendations for home activities to your observations. By encouraging parents to follow up on their child's work with home experiences, you bring parents in as partners in the learning and evaluation process. For example, you might write:

Megan writes best when she has a clear sense of her audience. To capitalize on this, you might encourage her to write letters or e-mail messages to out-of-town friends or relatives.

Chad has recently moved into reading chapter books. You might ask him to read a book from the Henry and Mudge series to you.

Although Terry struggled when we began our unit on decimals, his confidence has increased. To give him a chance to practice, you might ask him to help you keep track of the costs while you're grocery shopping.

If you're not sure what to recommend for a student, you might consider starting with the students' own goals. If you ask your students to set their own goals for work in the next quarter—in a sense, to write their own recommendations—you might decide to organize your report card comments around these goals. Using the goals as a starting point will help you decide what to focus on, as well as provide feedback to the students about how they're progressing toward those goals.

Simple Models for Change

At the school where Kelly used to teach, writing position papers was a part of the tenth-grade English curriculum. Because the term *position paper* was a new one to them, students were always nervous when the project was introduced. Only when Kelly shared her own piece in progress, a tongue-in-cheek, two-page argument about why Oprah Winfrey should run for president, did students realize that the assignment was manageable. They needed an attainable model before they could begin work comfortably.

Teachers writing report card narratives are no different. Since our own report cards from our student days rarely resembled those we are asked to produce as teachers, we sometimes need a model of what narratives might look like, a sense of what might be appropriate to include in them. When we see a few samples of well-written report card narratives (and realize how concise some of them can be), many of us breathe the same sigh of relief that Kelly's students did. For this reason, we have included here a few examples of fine written assessments that can fit in that two-inch comment space.

Judy Kenney wrote the following sentences about Ginny, a second grader, on a January report card:

> Ginny has been enjoying the unit on folklore we've been doing this past semester. After reading all the myths and fairy tales, she thought up her own detailed, creative story called "The Sandy Colored Cyclops." She worked on a second version of this with Vicki and they seemed to have a good time adding a few more gory details!

Judy's assessment is brief, but it suggests a wealth of information about Ginny as a learner: Ginny connects her reading with her writing, she understands the conventions of a fairy tale well enough to borrow them for her own work, and she enjoys collaborating on projects with her peers.

The following description of a third grader's science learning is similarly brief, but it reports a vivid slice of academic success to the student's parents:

> Recently we have been investigating water during science time. Although Robert has had a hard time articulating his learning in writing, he sketched a drawing of the water cycle in his science journal that demonstrated his understanding with elaborate details. As he was working, I heard him clearly explaining the difference between evaporation and condensation to Wally, his seatmate. During independent reading, he also chose to reread *Waterdance,* a picture book about the water cycle that I read aloud.

This paragraph acknowledges Robert's struggle with writing—something of which his parents are undoubtedly already aware—while highlighting his artistic and verbal communication skills. It cites three specific classroom events to demonstrate Robert's investment in the water unit, providing his parents with enough information that they can ask Robert informed questions about his learning.

During the year Dory Green was a first grader, her teacher Joanne Thompson wrote brief narratives on her reading and writing on three occasions (see Figure 3.2). Since conferences were held during the third term—a fact Joanne clearly notes on the report card—no narrative assessment was written at that time. Even though Joanne's assessments consist of only a few sentences, they include several concrete examples of classroom events. After the first term, she describes Dory and a classmate trying to puzzle out the meaning of the word *thresh* and provides a little snippet of Dory's speech: "Let's go on, we know she did something to that wheat." Dory's parents also get a sense of her improvement over time, as Joanne reports in Term 2 that Dory has "discovered the world of 'chapter books'" and she "is also beginning to rewrite and revise independently before asking for a conference with an adult." Both developments are new since the beginning of the year.

Each of these teacher-writers has paid attention to the small, concrete details that signal deep-seated growth and engagement in learning. In the following extensions, we provide some ways to help you gather more details, and think about what needs to be written in your report card comments.

EXTENSIONS

1. Create a notetaking form.
Include all of your students, and use it periodically (see Figure 3.3 for an example of fifth-grade teacher Gail Gibson's notes during library time). Make it a goal to write something specific about every student at the end of the week. Sometimes, having a list of everyone's name can jog your memory and allow you to remember details that might otherwise be lost.

2. Do the "What's Valued in Evaluation?" activity.
This is a good exercise to do alone or with colleagues, to think about what language and insights for report card comments might be most effective.

FIGURE 3.2   Joanne Thompson's quarterly narratives

Dory Green   **Mapleton Elementary School**
                                   Grade 1, Joanne Thompson

First Term
Reading:
Dory is in the early stage of reading. She is able to read independently and is very often seen doing so. She is expecting to get meaning from what she reads and often rereads if the text is not making sense to her. She was able to find a misprint in *Noisy Nora* after I had read it as it should have been printed. She predicts very well and enjoys or does not enjoy certain books. While reading *Little Red Hen* with a classmate, I overheard both of them discussing if the word "threshing" might not be "trashing." They were not able to come up with "threshing" but they knew that "trashing" did not make sense. "Let's go on, we know she did something to that wheat."
Writing:
Dory is in the early stage of writing. She fully understands that writing can convey meaning. She is able to write lists, sentences, complete thoughts, and labels very well. She is able to take risks with spelling and is coming very close to conventional form. Her writing is very readable. We will work on punctuation as the need arises this term.

Second Term
Reading:
Dory continues to show that she is able to read more difficult text. She is beginning to become interested in different kinds of text. She is able to use the strategies that enable her to read easier text on this more difficult text. She has discovered that world of "chapter books" (like the big people books). She has good comprehension of what she reads. She is humble about her ability to read and is always ready and willing to help any of her peers.
Writing:
Dory is rapidly becoming a fluent writer. She is writing with ease and is becoming more adept with writing conventions. She realizes the many purposes of writing. The display of voice in her writing sets her above the expected level for first grade. We are now working on punctuation and editing for spelling. She is also beginning to rewrite and revise independently before asking for a conference with an adult.

Third Term
Due to conferences having been just previous to this reporting term, there are no written comments.

Fourth Term
Reading:
Dory is in the fluent stage of reading. She is interested in different types of text. She continues to work on strategies and uses them to decode text. Many times she and two of her peers are heard discussing books that they have read and recommending them to each other. She continues to choose books that are challenging to her and still continues to delight in the discovery that she is able to read. I hope that she does not discover that she has all the elements of a reader too soon. She is finding it such a discovery now.
Writing:
Dory is also in the fluent stage of writing. She definitely has gained control of most of the writing conventions and is writing with ease. She has a fantastic sense of story development and uses her own voice in everything that she writes. She is editing and doing some revising willingly when it does not make sense to the reader. She accepts suggestions willingly. She has published numerous pieces this year and is always ready to start a new project in writing.

FIGURE 3.3   Gail Gibson's whole-class notes

Date 9/16

Activity _First Visit to Library — Choosing Books_

Student	Tally	Discussed choices with me	Asked for help	Notes
Andrea	I			asked for help finding a mystery - Doll House Murders
Julie				absent
Randy	I			Chose bk. on music for B. - 'a assignment - read alone
Bobby	II			browsed shelves (fiction)
James				nonfiction - Eyewitness sharks - Pele (soccer)
Jill			?	help finding a fantasy → Watership Down
Monty				picture book - Aesop Fable
Peter			?	asked for help finding White Mountain
Gale				(band) went later - Anne of Green Gables
Lorie	I			Littlest Angel + another picture book
Lynn	I		?	picture broke - showed them to me
Hannah	I			sequel to Best X-mas Pageant ever
Devon	II			"strong a band x choosing bks"
Leigh	I		?	help w/ C.C. - building - wants to build a fort
Billy			?	(band) → no bks → brochure under architecture (!)
Mick				shared Eyewitness w/ D. - Mummies
James				3-D bks - reading names of animals - "my eye hurt"
Brian				bought bk from me last rd.
Luke	II			nonfiction - read them before
Don	I			a picture b/c - read them before (band)
Deanna	I			picture b/cw (band)
Kristina				footnote - explained call #'s nonfiction
Frank	I		?	(band)
Ken				
Toby				
Jack				

(circled note) asked me to read me an dope L.", + H / had read to / reading partner!

Asked for to read! time to read

long word card catlog
chose sport + nonfiction
given chose picture books
sequel + gene?

Skills to check:
- C. Catalog - call #'s
- finding biographies

WHAT'S VALUED IN EVALUATION?

Parents	Teachers	Students	Administrators

1. _____

2. _____

3. _____

4. _____

List four different things that each group in your school values when it comes to assessment of students. For example, under administrators you might list "High test scores" or "Enjoyment of school." Under teachers you might list "Working well in classroom community," and so on. Once you have four values listed for each group, put stars next to common values across groups (e.g., you might decide both teachers and parents value students reading on their own for pleasure) and put X's next to the most contentious differences (e.g., administrators might value high test scores, and teachers might value assessment that doesn't involve standardized measures). Think about what these differences mean for the comments you make on your report cards. How can you be true to your values and beliefs and still honor those of others in your reporting? This is a useful activity for an inservice day.

3. Take a look at the report card you use now.

Decide if any preparation will be needed before you change your report card comments. You may want to design and attach a grid sheet with an explanation at the top of what your comments are for. You may also want to draft a cover letter to parents, explaining your new system. Make sure you let parents know that you are in the process of changing the way you write evaluation comments, to prepare them for further changes as you experiment and find what works best for you.

4 BEGINNINGS AND ENDINGS

A Grand Opening. A first tooth. A kiss. A wave good-bye. A last class. An airplane fading in the sky.

Our lives are marked by beginnings and endings. In the rituals of the things we do day after day, we look for those moments which are starting points, or the final link in a long chain of events. We hold those images—their sight, smell, taste, and feel—close to us as we move through our daily routines.

It's no wonder that writers take such care to craft strong leads and endings. A fresh lead can begin a piece with a burst of energy that carries the writing to completion. Those first few words help any reader know if it's worth the time and energy to continue reading. And the last words often determine if the writing will be memorable, staying with a reader long after the book or magazine is put away.

We talk a lot in education about the need for good assessment, for instruments and strategies that get at the heart of what students are learning. But we talk very little about how the difference between a good assessment and a mediocre one is often the quality of the writing. This is especially true with narrative evaluation. If you want to be a better evaluator, you need to improve your writing. This isn't as difficult as it may seem, if you focus on the parts of the written narrative that are most critical and easiest to improve.

The lead is the most important part of any piece of writing. Good leads sing, pulling readers immediately into your classroom and the learning of one student. Often you have to write through a lot of tone-deaf incidents, ideas, and observations to get to the lead that is best for any one narrative. And you also have to be merciless to your own writing, whacking off as much of the beginning of your drafts as is necessary to find a good lead. In this chapter, we'll provide a few simple tips to help you develop stronger leads, and close your evaluations in ways that make the writing endure for readers.

Writing Powerful Leads

Like the telling classroom incidents you noted in the last chapter, telling leads can be found throughout any classroom. Once you know what you're looking for, great leads for assessment narratives almost write themselves. It's a process of learning to recognize leads in the midst of teaching. The following types of leads have been used effectively in narratives by teachers in widely different situations.

Dialogue Leads

Dialogue provides many lively leads in writing. A dialogue lead to an evaluation narrative serves two purposes: it puts readers immediately into the classroom, and it captures a student through his or her own language. Pat Rawson shows the spirit of a child in this narrative evaluation lead:

"You're supposed to say 'rabbit rabbit' today to bring us good luck this month!" So Melanie informs us during circle time. On a daily basis she shares her wide range of information with us, from "Oil is poisonous to fish" to "Turtles came from a long time before the dinosaurs."

It's important in a dialogue to begin with words that struck you as you listened to your students. If the words were striking to you, chances are they may also grab readers' attention. Some teachers choose instead to tape-record small groups of students when they aren't in the groups' presence. This enables them to listen to the tapes at their leisure—on the commute home or while doing other tasks—to find natural dialogue that captures a student's learning.

Circular Lead/Close

The *circular lead/close* is easiest to develop once an evaluation narrative is completed. When you've almost finished a narrative, you merely look back at the lead. Can you also begin the writing with those closing words? A circular lead/close is a favorite of many teachers writing evaluations once they try it, because the writing feels like it has come full circle, and it is such a tidy way to end. Debbie Folsom captured her student's enthusiasm for learning with this lead:

> I love school. It is fun!!!
> This was the writing in the voice bubble that accompanied Gary's photo displayed on our hallway bulletin board, including 42 exclamation marks. Gary is excited to be a part of our class, and this carries through to everything he does.

After documenting Gary's learning over the next two pages, Debbie closes with these words:

> Gary is a fun student. I enjoy having him as part of the class!!

And, of course, she closes with 42 exclamation points.

When you find yourself summarizing and at a loss for finishing an assessment, look back to the first few words you wrote. There is often a way to circle back to that idea, once you try.

The Climax Lead

Writer Becky Rule says it's a good idea to pick up your readers by the scruff of the neck and drop them into the heart of a conflict. Every piece of writing has a climax to it, though the climax doesn't always come at the very end of the piece. In writing an evaluation narrative, think about the moment of greatest achievement for a student during the term, and then move the description of that incident to the beginning of your draft. These *climactic leads* grab readers' attention. Who wouldn't want to read Amanda Hersey's evaluation of Melissa Kerrigan, after this opener:

> ". . . and the little girl watched so much t.v. that her eyes turned to glass." Melissa beamed as she read her story to the whole class. Melissa takes great pride in her accomplishments . . .

Randa Viitala chooses to lead with the moment her student found an item during a mock archeological dig:

> "I feel something!" was the cry heard from Kevin Hall as he began digging. He worked very carefully, uncovering each buried item and brushing off any excess sand with his brush. After examining one artifact he exclaimed, "Holy moley, what's this? Fossils. It has fossils!"

The reaction you want to receive from parents and colleagues when they read these narratives is, "Yep. I know that kid." These moments of greatest insight and pleasure experienced by the student reveal the core nature of that learner.

Metaphorical Leads

When we can't describe exactly what something is, we tend to describe what it is like. The *metaphorical lead* compares the student or her learning to something else, in a way that conveys the essence of her experience. Consider the following:

The Ocean

The ocean
is cold and sometimes
it's warm
it's quiet and nice and
an unforgettable sight
with a windy day and
a windy night.
                    Liz Caron

It's quiet and nice and an unforgettable sight to see Liz at work with her writing and reading. Whether she is working by herself, or more likely, with another girl, Liz is always diligently striving to express herself in more and better ways.

What is the child before you like? Deep and quiet as the ocean? As animated as a puppy? Often you need look no further than children's language to find your metaphors. Young students are natural metaphor makers about their work and learning. You could even give them some stems to work with, such as "I work as hard as a _____" or "My science log is like a _____" to see what metaphors they come up with to describe themselves, and then develop leads starting with their ideas.

Anecdotal Leads

Re-creating a scene from your classroom that marks a high point in the student's term is an effective way to bring readers into your classroom, and the learning of a particular child. Martha Winn captures a student at work with others in her lead:

It is first thing in the morning, and only a few children have arrived. They are writing sentences or poems to cut out and paste on our Reading House. The morning theme song, "Oh

What a Beautiful Morning" is on, and we are busily preparing for the day.

Suddenly, something catches my eye, and I glance up to see Morgan not only singing, but hop-skip-jumping to the music while she pastes her "I love houses" sign onto the Reading House.

Martha brings this scene to life with just the right language, especially the invented verb "hop-skip-jumping." Many good classroom incidents have something physical in the center of them, like that large box or the child digging in Randa's archeology lead. An object that is striking, and not normally seen in the classroom, can immediately draw readers into your writing.

The Unexpected Lead

Surprise your readers. Kim Wright begins her narrative with a quote from Mom: "'Stanley is eleven years old going on forty,' his mother commented." How is he old? In talk? In demeanor? In relationship with peers? You want to read on to solve the mystery.

Julie Bishop tells readers to expect the unexpected in looking at Taylor:

When you first look into our camp if you expect to see Taylor sitting cross-legged in our group circle or reading a book sitting up you probably won't. Taylor is the young boy who generally will be found lying down on his belly or back. You may even find him crouched like a frog, ready to leap, during our morning group time.

Leading with Student Work

Finally, the most effective lead is often the easiest to write. Beginning with a sample of student work draws parents and other teachers in and it highlights the importance of tracing student growth through actual artifacts. Many teachers comb through journals and student self-evaluations to find just the right beginning for their assessments. Chances are, if something is showing up repeatedly in a child's work, others at home are probably hearing about it, too. Kathy Salkaln started her assessment with this excerpt from Cindy's journal:

"I really want to get some fish. I really, really, really, really, want to get some fish," Cindy wrote for several days in her journal.

In her evaluation of a young learner, Kim Wright chose to begin with a drawing and some writing:

[Jail Picture Here] "this is a person inside jail for reading." And this is an example of Adam's humor and reveals how he is establishing a sense of belonging. I had just spent a considerable amount of time conferencing with Adam. After the conference, he seemed much more relaxed. He went back to his desk, and joined in the "goings on" of the boys in his group, one of whom was cartooning with illustrations and dialogue such as this. Adam drew the picture and gave it to me.

Adam stays on the perimeter until the situation or environment looks safe. Upon first impression, he seems aloof and not interested, but actually he wants to be and enjoys being involved.

Notice the way Kim uses the writing as a springboard to reveal something about Adam's work style and personality as a learner. While the student work sample should be interesting by itself, the ones that work best in narratives lead naturally into these kinds of global statements about students in many settings.

ENDINGS

With endings, it's best to begin by teaching you how *not* to end your narrative. There are countless wonderful ways to close an assessment, depending upon your purpose and audience. But there are three horrible endings that rear their heads again and again in narrative assessments. If you learn to recognize these ending blunders in your own writing, you are more likely to be able to craft unique closings.

The first mistake is *not trusting that what you have written says what you want it to say.* When this happens, teachers repeat the key points of their assessments, bludgeoning them in the process. Trust that you've done a good job representing your points earlier in the writing, and ruthlessly cross out any repetition.

Teachers also make the error of *reverting to chronology* in their narratives, taking readers on a not-so-enlightening "and then we did this and it was so interesting" tour of the curriculum during the semester. Limit your explanations of curriculum chronology to a paragraph or two early in the narrative, and try to pull out just a few examples or incidents to represent the learning of each student.

The last variation for a failed close to a piece is the *catch-all ending,* used when the narrative writer doesn't know where to begin to tidy up the loose ends in the piece. If you find yourself closing with common generic statements like "In sum, Susan is a delightful student who is a pleasure to have in class daily," push yourself to eliminate these vague generalities that readers will skim through and that weaken the impact of your observations.

We find the best way to end narratives is with specific recommendations for the readers. In this way, assessments are not unlike oral conferences with students about their learning. We never leave a conference without making sure that we and the student have a good sense of what will come next. After detailing how and what a student learned in a given period of time, it's essential that parents and other readers be brought into the process of supporting this learner. We encourage teachers to close each evaluation with a small number (five or less) of very specific suggestions or strategies for parents to work on with their children.

Remember that narrative evaluations may be a new concept to parents, and the recommendations at the end of these narratives may seem intimidating to them. Parents may view their perfectly normal child as in need of serious remedial help if your recommendations exhort them to work at home with their child. That's why it's important to make it clear to parents—through a cover letter, previous oral and written communication, or even within the narrative—that they are partners and co-teachers in their child's learning. This will alleviate their concerns about the recommendations and their ability to carry them out.

Unfortunately, most evaluations end with very global, not specific, statements about what the student needs to do: "Aaron should spend more time reading at home." "Marcia needs to learn how to work independently." These aren't notions that most parents would disagree with when reading about their child. But such observations give little insight into how parents and teachers can work together to meet that goal.

Look again at the statement, "Aaron should spend more time reading at home." If a conscientious parent reads this recommendation, she might require Aaron to read more before he goes to bed, or find time over the next few weeks for a bit more reading. But, really, what child couldn't benefit from more reading at home? It's a catch-all recommendation that will be ignored by many parents. Contrast this recommendation with one from Kimberley Wright, given to Adam's parents:

> Adam enjoys the R. L. Stine books. Other books that Adam might be encouraged to read include horror, friendship, and humorous books such as the John Bellair series, including *The House With the Clock in the Walls, Farmer Boy* by Laura Ingalls Wilder, and *Sideways Stories from Wayside School* by Louis Sacher. Suggestions from science and technology include the "Eyewitness" series published by Knopf and *The Way Things Work* by David McCaulay.

Kim shows she knows who this child is, and what books he might enjoy next. The parents have a list of authors to take to the library or suggest to their child when they visit a bookstore.

In recommendations like "Marcia needs to work independently," the parent might guess that Marcia needs to spend more time alone, away from peers. But Marcia will only be successful as a learner if she has some strategies for working alone. Contrast this recommendation with one from Julie Bishop, for Taylor:

> Encourage Taylor to use the three major meaning-making systems as he reads independently. He should ask himself the following questions as he reads:
> 1. Does it make sense?
> 2. Does it sound right?
> 3. Does it look right?
> While reading with parents, teachers, and others, Taylor should have these strategies encouraged and reinforced.

Julie gives readers ways to assist Taylor that are practical, concrete, and realistic.

Recommendations can also be developed from practices that have been successful for individual students in the classroom. In an assessment of Jon, a struggling writer, seventh-grade English teacher Suzy Kaback describes a specific strategy in enough detail that Jon's parents might be able to help him in the same way at home:

> Throughout the winter we worked on writing essays, which was a challenge for Jon. A strategy that helped him organize his ideas was verbally explaining his thesis statement and supporting evidence. I would take notes on Jon's oral explanation, and he would use these notes in drafting his essay. This system allowed him to break down the task into manageable parts, rather than struggling with expression while developing his thoughts.

Not only does Suzy specify how the strategy works, but she also provides a rationale for why it is helpful to Jon.

When writing recommendations at the end of a narrative, ask yourself these questions:

1. Will the reader be able to do this immediately?

2. Am I using any terms the reader won't understand?

3. Is the recommendation specific for this child, or is it something that could be written about any child this age?

The narrative by Mary Bagley (in Figure 4.1) shows how strong leads and endings are the heart of a powerful narrative. Her narrative is not long, but it is clearly rooted in one child's work. There is no generic fluff, and it's all built from observations and assessments Mary did of the student in reading and writing. The middle sections of this evaluation are particularly effective, and the principles Mary uses to craft those sections will be the topic of the next chapter.

EXTENSIONS

1. Review students' journals or writing folders.
Use tape flags or Post-its to mark possible leads. Share what you're doing with students, and maybe they'll help you find them.

2. Keep a lead list.
Set aside a page in your planbook or monitoring notebook to jot down possible leads as you encounter them during the term. This way, they'll be easily accessible to you when it comes time to write narratives later.

3. Get a sense of the possibilities available to you.
Pick a child you know well and generate as many leads as you can for his or her narrative, using the lead categories presented in this chapter and any others you can think of. Share them with a partner and discuss the benefits and costs of beginning with each of them.

FIGURE 4.1   Mary Bagley's case report

Case Report for Jasmine Hewett
Prepared by Mary H. Bagley

Our group of children was creating a volcano from a large cardboard box. A brainstorming session resulted in ideas for lava flows, flames, smoke, and falling rocks. Colored papers were placed on the table and the markers and scissors began to fly. Jasmine and another child were dispatched to bring the big box into the center of the room. As they shuffled along with their burden, they turned to me and said, "Mrs. Bagley, *this* is team work!"

Lots of distinctive, active verbs in the lead. Very concrete.

Working as part of a team is something Jasmine truly enjoys. I've watched her collaborate on writing, share a book with a friend, and use free time to draw pictures with special chums. She's always the first to offer a helping hand and to volunteer suggestions and comments during a group discussion. Many times I have witnessed her helping other children as they attempted to spell something in their writing or figure out a word in a book.

Mary provides examples of 3 different situations that support her assertion.

When I discussed reading with Jasmine, she told me about her Reading Recovery experience and the good reading practices she learned there. While I watched and listened to her read, I saw those practices being used. She always scans the pictures on the page to gather information about the text. She knows how to use punctuation to guide her expression and the flow of the words. She rereads phrases to correct them when they do not make sense. And she uses clues in the rest of the sentence to help figure out unknown words. She also notices words that are included in the illustrations and reads them aloud as well. When reading a book about the rainforest, Jasmine used what she knew about the forest to figure out the words in the story. When she retells the stories she reads, she includes many of the details and all of the important events.

With this detail, Mary supports her colleagues' work.

Lots of specific strategies that parents might look for while reading at home.

An example of a specific reading experience.

During writing time, Jasmine created a number of poems. Her subjects have included eyes, dogs, and birds. She especially enjoyed publishing her poetry on colorful posters. Together we produced a very large eye, complete with lashes, and copied her eye poem on the pupil. She likes to collaborate on writing projects as well. She and a

FIGURE 4.1　Continued

friend wrote a long piece about birds and horses. They kept adding chapters as they searched for information in our bird collection. With another friend, she worked on a piece about dogs. Jasmine willingly shared with the group her knowledge of webbing, a pre-writing activity that helps the writer organize thoughts about a piece. Jasmine's writing folder contains many webs, and she puts this practice to good use as she writes her poems and stories.

Mary doesn't assume that parents will know the term "webbing." She provides a jargon-free definition within the sentence.

Recommendations for Jasmine's further literacy learning:

1. Jasmine has shown an interest in poetry. There are many wonderful collections of poetry to share that are available in area libraries and book stores. These include:

> The New Kid on the Block by Jack Prelutsky
> The Random House Book of Poetry selected by Jack Prelutsky
> Side by Side, Poems to Read Together collected by Lee Bennett Hopkins

Recommended titles are common ones, easy for parents to find. The last book connects to Jasmine's obvious enjoyment of social literacy activities.

2. After Jasmine has finished a poem, she likes to publish it in a creative, colorful way. A variety of papers, markers, and writing implements would encourage her continued success with writing poetry.

3. As Jasmine loves to share reading and writing with a partner, all opportunities to do so will keep her using the good practices she has developed. Buddy reading (reading with a partner and taking turns reading parts of the story) is a valuable way for Jasmine to share books and stories.

These recommendations build from the positive, from things Jasmine is already doing well. They are a natural outgrowth of the observations described in the middle of the narrative.

5 In the Zone: Finding the Right Details

The *ecotone* is a term used by ecologists to describe the zone between two distinct environmental systems. It might be the boundary area between the ocean and dry land or between farmland and the rocky cliffs that begin a bordering mountain range. These ecotones are of special significance to scientists, because it is here that unexpected new vegetation and life forms flourish. If you want to know how an ecosystem works, you spend a lot of time focusing on its boundaries.

The concept of the ecotone is helpful when thinking about what details are most important to include in narrative assessments. Learning is really about moving between boundaries, about the changes that occur as students grasp new academic and social concepts. In choosing what to put between the strong leads and endings described in the last chapter, teachers look to the ecotones in each student's work—the examples of shifts in knowledge, attitude, and final products that signify growth.

This ecotone in learning is often described as the "zone of proximal development." Based upon the work of Vygotsky (1978), this zone is the place where students can understand and do more with assistance from a teacher, a parent, or a more experienced peer than they can do alone. These are the skills they are in the process of understanding and using. The few details you choose to include in the narrative should aim to demonstrate where this zone of learning is, and how teachers, parents, and peers can help the learner grow within it.

Narratives are less useful when they work only in the two areas outside of the zone of proximal development. Many assessments merely celebrate what a child can do well or, worse, catalogue all the inadequacies of the student. Evaluation narratives are a vital tool for helping students grow socially and academically only if they include clear snapshots of those zones where the student is ripe for growth and change.

It's better to choose a few specific incidents or insights to share than plump up a narrative with lots of broad, meaningless observations about a student's achievement and personality. We push teachers to write no more than two-page narratives to parents, with many teachers opting for a page or less. If you've included a one- or two-paragraph description of activities the whole class is engaged in, and you've also found a strong lead and ending for each of your narratives, there is room for only a couple observations about each student's zone of learning. Many teachers choose to comment briefly on each subject area, with a specific anecdote or example from the area the student is working hardest in at that time.

Consider this paragraph from a two-page evaluation narrative written by Kim Wright about a fifth-grade boy:

Adam is much more relaxed in an informal setting. He enjoys team games and free play. He is more at ease on the playground than he is in the classroom. On the playground, he is assertive and joins in the activity on his own. In the classroom, Adam tends to hang back and waits to be invited to join in. The more structured and unfamiliar the setting and activity, the more uncomfortable and inhibited he becomes. Adam's comfort level determines the amount of participation or work that gets done. He uses a lot of nonverbal communication to try to make connections with others. He looks at others to let them know he wants to join in or be part of the group. Adam needs to be encouraged to speak and not rely on nonverbal communication techniques. Adam cooperates well with his classmates. Once he establishes a friendship, he becomes much more at ease and loosens up. Adam is more willing to share when he is comfortable. For example, after a few days in school, Adam started bringing books to share from home such as *Calvin and Hobbes* and *Goosebumps.*

Kim shows the boundary where Adam might move next in his learning. She highlights where his social skills are most evident—on the playground—by giving concrete examples of Adam's assertiveness. Then, she shows how Adam's behavior shifts in the classroom. The implication is clear: Adam needs to move some of those social skills from the playground into the classroom. But he will need assistance in reaching this goal, and Kim expects to work with his parents in helping him become more assertive.

While parents and colleagues may feel confident about helping children develop social skills, they are less at ease about their role in helping students grow academically. Teachers also need to consider the parents' zone of learning when writing narratives. Professional jargon or vocabulary can distance parents from their child's work. For alternatives, consider this passage from Kathy Salkaln, written in a two-page narrative about a third-grader's reading:

Liz has read portions of two books this week: *Super Fudge* by Judy Blume, and *Hannah,* by Gloria Whelan. In both cases she was able to retell many details and the general plot of what she had read. Words that she miscues (words that Liz uses in place of what is actually written) are often words that are not in her vocabulary (for example, the word "privy"). Her miscues show that she depends on visual clues most of the time for decoding. For example, she read "combining" for "combing" and "thought" for "though." Less frequently, she relies on context clues (using the rest of the sentence to discover the word through meaning). She does not stop herself and reread a sentence or paragraph when it doesn't make sense. When we go back and reread a sentence or paragraph, she is able to say the correct word when she looks closely at its context. When reading a selection from the book *Hannah,* she depended upon graphophonemic (visual) clues 90 percent of the time, syntax (using the same part of speech) 80 percent of the time, and meaning 20 percent of the time. A fluent reader will use all three strategies, or ways of decoding a word. However, her retellings demonstrate that she comprehends much of what she reads.

We have worked on the strategy of skipping an unknown word, reading the end of the sentence or paragraph, and then returning to see if we can figure out the word in the context of what comes before and after. Liz is able to make valid predictions based upon what she has just read.

Through her miscues, Liz has demonstrated that she does not always read word for word, but in "chunks," a sign of fluency. She makes miscues which do not interfere with the meaning (for example, "a" for "the"). I discussed her miscues with Liz to make her aware of the strategies she was using and should be using in her reading.

Throughout this passage, Kathy shows a sensitivity to her audience's level of understanding and knowledge of professional terms. She doesn't assume parents or colleagues will know the meaning of words like "miscue" or even "strategy," and so she includes simple definitions after any words that might confuse her readers. In addition, she backs up many of her points with the actual words Liz used in reading passages from books. Finally, rather than just stating that Liz is developing fluency as a reader, she gives an example of this fluency. Within the context of what Liz does well as a reader, Kathy conveys the zone of learning that can still be developed, which includes focusing on texts and words making sense.

One of the best ways to honor the work of students is to show their struggles to parents. This makes the successes more compelling. Barbara Libby wrote the following narrative about a seventh-grade student who has trouble working with others:

> During the past weeks Dan has been working hard to belong. When things went well, he would flash a wonderfully inclusive smile. When he had disappointments he would verbally articulate how he felt and sometimes "walk off" his feelings for a few minutes, then return to the group ready to try again. When his group made a video commercial, he eventually took responsibility for being the "sound man," a less active role than he had wanted, demonstrating his desire to be part of the group.
>
> Dan seemed most comfortable working in pairs. In those situations his graciousness and sense of humor were apparent. He did a fine job reading to and listening to a younger buddy twice each week. The first time we did this, he chose a book that was too long to hold the interest of the child and he had a disappointing experience. After that he chose shorter stories and made a visible effort to hold his buddy's attention, demonstrating his resilience.

Given that Dan is in seventh grade, we suspect his parents already know that he struggles in social settings and needs to develop strategies for working in groups. How much more helpful it is for parents to read about the ways their child learned from mistakes and used them to change his behavior successfully. Parents enjoy it when teachers tick off their child's successes; they can be discouraged by a laundry list of their child's failings. But they *learn* from seeing the moment their child learns—when the switch is turned on in their child's mind, and a compelling shift in behavior, thinking, or productivity occurs.

If you are looking for details to include in your narratives, look for student tensions, flubs, and misunderstandings. It is these break-through moments of learning that add zest to a narrative and provide clues for what students might be ready to learn next. Consider this detail Tracy Forbes included in describing second grader Terence during writer's workshop:

> "It helps me to play, then write." Because Terence is so thoughtful, he finds putting all of his ideas on paper to be a tremendous task. Combined with this, he experiences frustration with fine motor control. On one occasion, Terence desperately wanted to write his story and expressed his need to manipulate objects in order to write about them. Allowed the time and space to play with his pirate ship as he wrote, Terence was able to produce his most lengthy and creative piece in which he envisioned himself to be a pirate upon his ship. He was proud of this piece and read it aloud to classmates.

In technical terms, Tracy has shown that Terence is a "tactile" learner, a word she uses later in the narrative. Even more important, she shows that Terence has figured out he is a tactile learner, and knows that physically holding and manipulating objects will help him learn and work in the classroom.

It is also important to describe how students interact with their teachers or more experienced peers while working in their zone of proximal development. Steve Kaback included the following passage in an assessment of Brendan:

> Perhaps Brendan's greatest strength has been his zeal in pursuing new concepts until he fully understands them. He has asked sharp, insightful questions in class, at recess, in the hallways, and even in the dining hall at dinner. When he has had difficulty with homework assignments, he has been thorough and prompt in his make-up work. I applaud this kind of determination.

By listing the places where Brendan asked questions, Steve creates an image of a young man committed to getting help from his teacher. The reader also gets a peek at Brendan's work habits and his strategies for dealing with challenge.

A restaurant in our neighborhood proudly advertises a smorgasbord with over eighty items served daily. What they don't advertise is the quality of the items: lots of greasy fried potatoes, jello with mushy mini-marshmallows, limp green beans swimming in butter. When making choices about what to include in your narratives, choose quality over quantity. What would you rather eat: one hundred Twinkies or one really delicious thin slice of Sacher torte? Four trays of overcooked carrots or one truly fresh small Caesar salad? Don't lard your narratives with lots of insignificant details about students' learning. Instead, nourish your readers by placing them in the zone of each child's learning with a few strong examples and anecdotes. By experiencing the zone of their child's learning, parents can see most vividly what their child knows, and what she needs to learn next.

Extensions

1. Write small and say something big.
In *What a Writer Needs* (1993), Ralph Fletcher reminds us to write small to say something big. We think this is particularly good advice for writers of narratives. In Chapter 3, we advised you to make a list of descriptive adjectives to form an initial portrait of each student, then to collect anecdotal evidence to support your assertions. The same process can work backward as well. Pull a few examples of small, concrete observations of your students from your notes, then consider possible implications for each example. "Sherry read her piece during whole-class share today" might mean that shy Sherry's becoming more comfortable in the class community, or that she's finally finished a piece for publication after weeks of false starts, or that she's reached a point where she's ready to accept feedback from her peers.

2. Read a novel or a short story with rich characterization.
Pay careful attention to how the writer uses details to describe a character's physical appearance, voice, and attitudes. Borrow some of those strategies when writing your narratives. For starters, we recommend

Patricia MacLachlan's *Sarah, Plain and Tall,* Cynthia Rylant's *Missing May,* John Steinbeck's *Of Mice and Men,* and John Irving's *A Prayer for Owen Meany.* You can add to our list of books.

3. Eavesdrop for a few minutes on your students in a work situation.

Choose an activity in which students have the opportunity to interact with each other. Limit your notes to their speech, reported verbatim. You might also want to leave a tape recorder running while you aren't present in a group; then listen to the tape during your commute or while making dinner. These snatches of conversation can often illuminate a child's learning.

4. Defy all the suggestions we've made in this book.

Purposely write a narrative that glitters with generalities and drips with vagueness—it might help you get those tendencies out of your system when it comes time to write assessments for real, and it will certainly be worth a laugh. You might also write a wicked narrative including all the things it would be unprofessional to tell the parents of your most frustrating student (or a composite of several students). In our experience, these narratives are especially ripe for sharing, but do so in a soundproof room, and swallow the pieces of paper after you read your draft—we don't want this kind of thing to get out!

6 WRITING NARRATIVES IN BULK: WHEN YOU GOTTA LOTTA STUDENTS

Remember how old black-and-white movies showed the passage of time through a rapid flip of calendar sheets, with the pages sometimes flying off into the distance? That's how the passage of time in many middle level and high school classrooms feels—fast and always amid a flurry of white paper. Certain elements of the narrative writing process remain consistent for teachers of any grade level, elementary through college. But teachers who have many students face special constraints. This chapter is primarily for middle school and high school teachers whose class lists may total as many as 200 students and who must juggle the curriculum, student needs, and student assessment in creative ways. However, K–5 teachers with large classes may find useful information here as well.

The bad news if you teach middle school or high school students is that you have many more assessments to write than your primary school colleagues do. The good news is that your students are more capable of sharing those assessment responsibilities with you. Although it is ultimately your job to write evaluations about your students' learning, students themselves can play an integral role in that process. The following suggestions may help you enlist students as partners in your narrative writing to ease your own load and to aid students in becoming keener evaluators of their own work.

A System for Saving Student Work

The first thing you'll need in order to write high-quality narratives is a plan for saving and organizing student work. When you're writing narratives in bulk without the benefit of an organizational system students start to blur together and descriptions seem interchangeable, making it nearly impossible to say something different about each student. What's more, it's tough to write narratives dealing with students' growth over a term if you don't have concrete data from previous weeks or months. When teachers rely only on their memories, they tend to focus on what has happened most recently and forget how that compares to the student's performance at the beginning of the unit, quarter, or semester. Student work samples can serve as a mental anchor for you when you're making judgments about whether Chris has finally figured out mitosis or whether Jane's use of punctuation has improved. Having a large number of students makes it difficult, if not impossible, to rely solely on observational notetaking to track these changes, so preserving student artifacts becomes that much more important.

By encouraging you to save and review student work, we're not proposing that you become pack rats who file everything. While this advice is often given to elementary teachers, teachers who work with older students would soon find themselves overwhelmed by the sheer quantity of paper in the room. In fact, we strongly caution teachers with lots of students against filing anything at all. Instead, ask individual students to take responsibility for keeping track of their own work. Remember that a task requiring thirty seconds per student at the end of class will take you almost an hour if you do it for a hundred students after school. That's valuable time that you could spend writing.

We suggest providing students with manila folders or hanging files for storing their work samples. Initially, all completed student assignments can go into these folders. Give students a few minutes of class time every few weeks to sift through the papers they've accumulated and choose several that represent important aspects of their learning. They might want to include pieces that show improvement, represent a struggle they had, or reflect their best work. Many teachers ask students to write a few sentences about their selections on a Post-it or index card that can then be attached to the sample. While you will probably want to be directive about some things to include (e.g., all students must file their position papers or their water-quality lab reports), students should also make some choices about what work to save. Making their own selections will help them reflect on their own experiences and will reveal to you how they see themselves as learners in your class.

When you're ready to compose narratives, you can skim through the folders to get a sense of each student's work. The work samples will make your observations more specific and rooted in what the student has produced during the term.

DOUBLE-ENTRY SELF-EVALUATIONS

Another way to share responsibility with your students is to use their self-assessments as a catalyst for your own narratives. About six weeks into each trimester, middle school teachers Wally Alexander and Phil Cotty ask their students to complete detailed self-evaluations (see Figure 6.1). The students used class time to fill out these forms, which changed each trimester depending upon the curriculum and the time of year. Both teachers wrote their own comments in the wide margin, sometimes simply underscoring what the student had written and sometimes raising new issues and questions. In the final step of the process, parents provided feedback at the bottom of the form.

Figure 6.1 Wally Alexander's and Phil Cotty's midterm report

NAME Kristy _____ Midterm Report

Teacher Comments

Reader

I have read __5__ books so far this year.

I read an average of __60__ minutes each night at home.

The two best books I've read this year are:

The Giver   Lottery Rose

Solitary Rose

Very strong
reader. Chooses

I am prepared and participate well during reading conferences. 1 2 3 4 ⑤ challenging books

I really read during SSR. 1 2 3 4 ⑤

I listen carefully during Read-Aloud. 1 2 3 4 ⑤ (wh)

The thing I do best as a reader is:

Read fast. Know what I read.

I like to talk about my books.

← yes!

My greatest challenge as a reader is:

Read science textbooks.

Figure out new words.

Let's talk about
genre - especially
non-fiction (wh)

Writer

I complete three 1/2 page reflective journal entries each week. 1 2 3 4 ⑤

I try to make quality reflections in my journal. 1 2 3 4 ⑤

I work hard at editing my own writing. 1 2 3 4 ⑤

I often confer with classmates and teachers on my writing. 1 2 3 ④ 5

My best piece of writing this year was:

The Cliffs

Yes! Excellent!

The thing I do best as a writer is:

Think up ideas for my stories.

Help other people with their ideas.

My greatest challenge as a writer is:

Finishing things.

making changes

I agree.

Great idea. person!

yes - revision
Editing too!

Researcher (Block - science & social studies)

I work well with others. 1 2 3 4 ⑤

My work and time are well organized. 1 2 3 ④ 5

I am comfortable doing research on my own. 1 2 3 4 ⑤

I use a variety of resources well. 1 2 3 4 ⑤

My favorite resources to find information are:

Internet. magazines.

Interviews.

Good on computer.

The thing I do best as a researchers is:

Read. Ask questions I

know where to look for answers

My greatest challenge as a researcher is:

Take notes and put them

together in a draft.

We'll work on
this. It's part
of the next
unit.

Figure 6.1   Continued

Computer User

I have used the computer to do the following things this year (circle):
(Word Process)   Spread Sheet
(Telecommunication)   HyperCard
(Research)   Other _____

I use a computer about __5__ hours per week.

The thing I do best on the computer is:
Internet,
    I can find stuff.

Good skills, especially Internet

My greatest challenge as a computer user is:
Typing fast. Hypercard.

I'll help with Hypercard if you want. (WA)

Mathematician

I worked seriously on math inquiries:
(names, 36 groups, standards, place value, number systems)   1 2 3 4 ⑤
I ask for help repeatedly when I need to.   1 2③4 5
I hand in my work on time, neat and complete.   1 2③④5   ✓
I work hard to communicate fully and clearly.   1 2③④5
I develop strategies to solve problems.   1 2③4 5

The thing I've done best in math is:
Add and subtract. I hate
word problems.   ✓

I have dealt with changes this year by:
I liked the textbooks. I didn't want to
change. I talked to other kids and
my mom.

{ Reluctant, but coming along.

The area I need to improve the most is:
I need to get better at math. I don't like it. ~~Maybe~~

To improve in this area I need to: Maybe I need to ask more questions.
I need to read more kinds of stuff. I need to work on
m y word problems in math. I need to pay attention
in math, and work harder too.

{ I agree. We need to focus here.

Read your reflective journal carefully. What are some of your recurring concerns or themes?
① Books. I like when we write about books.
② math. How it changed.
③ Soccer ④ what I like in school ⑤ Computers.   ✓

Parent comments:
Kristy's reading this year more than ever. She's on the internet all the time
at home, so we're glad she's using that skill for research at school!
Although she was initially resistant to the changes in math, she seems
to be comfortable now.   **Parent sign here:** _Jeff Hagaburg_

Wally and Phil discussed these double-entry assessments with individual students during workshop time before the kids brought them home to their parents. The discussions provided a springboard for subsequent evaluation conferences between teachers and students, and the self-evaluations became significant pieces to include in students' portfolios, which were assembled at least three times a year. When you are just beginning to write narratives, you may find it easier and quicker to respond to a student's self-assessment and fill in any gaps you see than it is to generate the entire document from scratch.

Conferences as Pre-writing

You may also want to consider scheduling evaluation conferences with students a week or two before you begin to write your assessments. Prior to meeting with you, students might prepare responses to prompts such as the following:

- What was the highlight of the term for you as a learner?

- What was the hardest thing you did in this class this term?

- What represents your best work of the term?

- What goals do you have for yourself as a writer over the next six weeks?

As long as you set clear expectations and stick to a schedule, these conferences can be brief, lasting no longer than five minutes per student. Consider scheduling them about two weeks before your narratives are due, during a couple of classes when students are working independently. This way, you'll have time to confer with individual students without scheduling extra meetings. If you take good notes, you may find that students are actually writing pieces of their narratives for you as they speak. If you ask them to submit written notes, you'll have another data source that you can return to as you write.

CARVING OUT TIME TO WRITE

Chances are good that your biggest concern about writing narratives in bulk is *time*. In Chapter 2, we recommended that you start small, choosing a single class for your first batch of narratives rather than trying to write about all of them. We also advised beginning your assessments with a whole-class description that stays the same for each student—a practice we think is especially appropriate for middle and high school teachers. You might take your lead from Paul Ramsay, an intern working with John D'Anieri at Noble High School, who wrote about the principle assignments of the quarter and left spaces to fill in grades and comments for individual students (see Figure 6.2). This way, parents get a sense of what the class is doing as well as some details about their son's or daughter's progress. Once the overview is drafted, it takes only a minute to fill in information about individual students.

You might also follow the example of Wally Alexander and Phil Cotty. They designed a report card form that described their team-taught middle school classes in a few sentences, then left room for comments about students' performance in each of those classes (see Figure 6.3). Since Phil and Wally stored these descriptions on their personal computers, they changed both the descriptions and the format of the report card each term, depending on the curriculum themes. The following suggestions will also help make the job of writing assessments for large numbers of students more manageable.

We advise you to set conservative goals for the length of your assessments. In the beginning, a few sentences will be ample. Once you've decided on a length limit, stick to it. If you find you have more to say, consider writing more next time. It's better to write brief narratives of consistent quality than to write lengthier ones that deteriorate the further down the class list the name appears.

Some teachers find it helpful to set a time limit for their writing. They decide that they're going to spend no more than ten minutes per student on first drafts. As they become more proficient, they work to cut that time. We've heard of a few teachers who even use an egg timer

FIGURE 6.2   Progress report

Progress Report: Sophomore English
D'Anieri/Ramsay

The first unit of the second semester was on drama. We explored the qualities of drama and compared it to other forms of entertainment. To gain a firsthand, common experience, we went to the Seacoast Repertory Theatre to view Inherit the Wind. Students were assigned a position paper on "Who should determine what you learn?" which relates to the issues of academic freedom in the play. Finally, there was an exam on the qualities of drama and what took place at the play.

Inherit the Wind Exam: ___*nc*___

We continued working on the position papers from the first unit using the MEA scoring guide (students will have to take these their junior year) to shape their approach. Students were responsible for handing in a final draft.

Position Paper: ___*A-*___

The second unit dealt with storytelling. Students examined seven different stories that explained natural occurrences, taught morals or lessons, entertained, and/or preserved culture. We talked extensively about what the important qualities of storytelling were, and students were asked to reflect in their journals as well as write some small stories. There was an essay exam based on the stories we read, and the unit ended with an oral presentation in which each student told their peers a story.

Journals: ___*B-*___

Exam: ___*A-*___

Oral presentation: ___*A*___

Overall Grade: ___*nc*___

Comments: ___*Must make up exam*___

FIGURE 6.3   **Sample report card**

Sedgwick Elementary School
Middle Level Report Card

Student   Class   Date

Communication Skills (reading, listening, written language)

☐ Includes: essay writing; letter writing; reflective journal; open writing in writer's workshop; vocabulary; speaking; spelling; reading groups; personal reading; book extensions; organizations.

Mathematics (solving and creating problems; match reasoning and skills; communicating strategies)

☐ Units this term on algebra and geometry.

French (language exercises; pronunciation; songs; dialogue; tests; projects; participation)

☐

Thematic Blocks (integrated science and social studies)

☐ Spring Term featured a block on Space, including a study of our solar system and the formation of the universe. We also did a block on Survival, that included animal adaptation, biomes, human survival, and survival skills including CPR, orienteering, and first aid. Block studies emphasized research skills, science content, test-taking, creative writing, word processing, readings, illustrated logs, and oral presentations.

☐ Chorus   ☐ Band   Days Absent _____
☐ Art   ☐ Physical Education   Days Tardy _____

Comments:

or alarm clock to help them keep track of time spent on individuals or classes of students. For some of you, a buzzer or ticking second hand will cause unnecessary stress. For others, it might be just the reminder you need to work quickly and move from draft to draft without agonizing over each one.

When teachers think about writing narratives in bulk, they often think they need to find large blocks of uninterrupted time. We have found our own needs to be just the opposite: we write only a few assessments at a time over a period of days, and we often write them during moments when a longer writing task would not fit. Look critically at your daily schedule for small pockets of time that could be used for writing. For example, you might make a habit of drafting a narrative during the first five or ten minutes of writing workshop each day or while monitoring study hall twice a week. We know a high school English teacher who recently made a goal of drafting her narratives orally, using a handheld tape recorder, during what she calls "wasted time": her forty-minute commute to and from work. She plans to transcribe these tapes loosely to get a beginning draft for her narratives.

What's important is that you find a way to write evaluations that fits easily into the fabric of your life and doesn't require you to sacrifice your family, exercise, or paying the bills just to complete your narratives. Building a writing routine into your schedule makes you much more likely to continue. And you'll probably be surprised by how quickly the completed drafts pile up, one by one, in five- or ten-minute chunks.

Making time to write narratives at the secondary level may necessitate some other changes in your practice. Notice that we've used the phrase, "making time," not "finding time." We don't believe that time is a fossil fuel, waiting to be discovered below the surface crust of our lives. Making time requires an active restructuring on teachers' part. You'll need to cut something else out of your schedule before you add writing narratives. Maybe you'll decide to require oral presentations rather than a written essay exam at midyear. Maybe you'll have more in-class conferences with student writers rather than the extensive comments you were writing on their papers at home. Maybe you'll require two projects a term rather than three, so you'll have that much more time to write.

You also might consider writing narratives at some time other than the official close of a quarter or semester. You've probably experienced what we like to call the "grading frenzy," that mad dash to respond to and tally all of the work (makeup or otherwise) that piles up before the term ends. Instead of trying to balance narratives with the traditional evaluation still required by many districts, you might choose to write your assessments during a time that is less stressful.

Consider writing assessments of projects, units, or particular assignments, rather than an entire term's or semester's work. In Kelly's literature seminar, high school juniors and seniors were required to complete two polished papers per quarter about their reading. She found it more natural to write letters directly to her students than to write third-person narratives about the quality of these papers (see Chapter 7 for a sample of these letters).

In addition, a narrative can be a particularly appropriate assessment for a project with a nonwritten product. For a unit that integrated history and literature, pairs of students in Kelly's tenth-grade English class scripted and performed imaginary meetings between important Civil War–era figures such as Sojourner Truth and John C. Calhoun. Although students submitted their notes, there was no formal written product to evaluate. The preparation for these projects, as well as the complexity, humor, and collaborative nature of the presentations, required a far greater response from the teacher than a letter grade or a tally of points. Instead, Kelly chose to write paragraph assessments addressed jointly to the pairs (see Figure 6.4).

One last caution: Some teachers who teach multiple sections of the same course—whether it's chemistry or seventh-grade language arts—choose to keep those classes on roughly the same schedule for units and projects. While this may save time in terms of planning, it can require you to write a large number of narratives concurrently (provided you decide to write them about more than one class at a time). Instead, you might consider staggering the starting dates of projects so that only one or two classes finish at once. You can then concentrate

FIGURE 6.4   Kelly Chandler's narratives about students' presentations

Rich Fairgate: Charles Sumner
Cole Gregory: Daniel Webster

Comments:
I felt like you were well-rehearsed; the first few moments seemed very smooth.
Rich seemed less nervous than Cole then, but Cole settled in well, especially
during the question-and-answer period. That's when I felt that Webster came
across most clearly. During the conversation itself, it might have been a good
idea to talk more about Webster's unwillingness to go to war. Rich as Sumner
said that was a chance he was willing to take; Webster did not feel the same way,
but Cole didn't tackle the point. Nonetheless, I felt that both of you had a
strong sense of your characters. I saw further evidence of that when Cole
coached Rudy from Period 3 a bit during study hall. No one in any of my other
sections knew Sumner as well as Rich. A few minor, picky complaints: "All men
are created equal" is from the Declaration of Independence, not the
Constitution—a small but not insignificant error. You also mentioned the
Kansas-Nebraska Act, which you would not have known about in 1850.
Otherwise, I was very pleased with your work. You should be proud of
yourselves.

Grade: A-

Shawn Davis: John Calhoun
Adam Nolan: Sojourner Truth

Comments:
Your conversation was very enjoyable and entertaining; I appreciated the
humor, as did your audience. Sojourner's costume…well, I'm not even sure
what to say about it. I thought you chose good quotations from actual sources,
although the first Calhoun one needed to be explained a bit more. I understood
it because I had read the whole speech, but the rest of the audience might not
have been aware of what you meant. Sojourner's question about imagining a
free country was a good one, and Calhoun used some nice rationalization to
squirm out from under it. You were a little on the short side, though, and
needed in a few places—the K/N Act and the Fugitive Slave Act—to develop
your ideas a little further. You also needed to rehearse a bit more since you
stumbled some as you were reading—Shawn in particular. Your answers to
questions were fine, but not terribly in depth. All in all, a good job that might
have reached a great job with a little more research and practice.

Grade: B

on completing a batch of assessments before the next wave of students turn in their essays or make their presentations.

Writing Narratives as Part of a Team

Many middle schools and an increasing number of high schools across the country have adopted a teaming model where a small number of teachers—usually between two and five—are primarily responsible for a core group of 40–150 students. In addition to the instructional benefits of coordinated curricula, teaming allows teachers to be more creative in their approaches to narrative writing. If you are fortunate enough to work in a setting like this one, here are some tips that may help you in your work.

1. Rotate the responsibility of writing narratives among team members.

Unless you are required to write individual reports for all of your students at certain intervals, you might want to consider alternating your narratives with a team member. Different students on your team could be on different reporting schedules. For example, Heather's parents might receive narratives about her performance in science and social studies during the first quarter, with her math and language arts teachers slated to write during the following term. Using this system, teachers are only responsible for writing half as many narratives in a given reporting period.

Instead of writing a reduced number of narratives each term, team members might also decide to coordinate when each will write about all of the students. Each teacher's long-term curriculum and assessment plans could help determine the schedule. If geometry students generally produce a major tessellation project during the second quarter, the math teacher might want to write her narratives then. If, six or seven weeks later, students script and perform a mock trial inspired by *Of Mice and Men,* this might be a perfect time for the English teacher to write about students' oral language development and creativity. In this way, parents consistently receive written information about their child's progress in at least one curricular area, but teachers are relieved of the pressure of producing narratives on multiple occasions. They need only gear up for the writing process once.

2. Allot some team time for writing, sharing, and editing narratives.

When Kelly taught high school English, her four-person interdisciplinary team met every other day for eighty minutes. Each term, the team devoted at least two or three meetings to writing the midterm progress reports that parents received four times a year. The narratives were written on a single sheet divided into four boxes, one for each teacher (see Figure 6.5).

3. Schedule a group brainstorming session.

Rather than dividing the report by subject or discipline, some teams may prefer to draft a single narrative to represent students' work across the team. These narratives might focus on certain skills or attitudes valued by all teachers on the team, such as collaboration, reflection, or organization. Team members might generate ideas together, taking notes, then the drafting of the narratives could be divided. Collective brainstorming can be especially helpful when writing about students whose behavior is challenging (working together can make it easier to focus the positive) or who tend to blend into the background (pooling your knowledge can often create a more complete picture).

EXTENSIONS

1. Write a cover letter to parents.

Individually or as part of a teaching team, draft a letter to parents about your plans for evaluation. Be honest with parents about the value of narrative assessment as you see it—and about the personal time and

FIGURE 6.5   A team progress report

SOPHOMORE TEAM 1 PROGRESS REPORT
ACADEMIC YEAR 1994-95

Name Nate Pullman
Quarter 1 2 (3) 4

Teacher Chandler
Subject English

Nate struggled to find a topic for his position paper but finally settled on euthanasia. He did a good job locating resources on his own but needs to work some more on directly quoting + citing information from them. His rough draft was well-organized but needs to be fleshed out in more detail. He's making steady progress with Anpao, his book for independent reading — sometimes he doesn't hear the bell!

Estimate of Grade B+

Teacher Gardner
Subject Biology

• Doing well with hands on activities at Blue River (collecting samples for water testing)
• Has a good understanding of pH and role it plays in watershed
• Labs are clearly written
• Performance on last test was 15 pts better than last one

Estimate of Grade B+

Teacher Jackson
Subject Geometry

Nate's quiz scores have improved since he began coming in for extra help. His homework is done consistently, although he is sometimes more interested in providing the answer than in explaining how he got it. His log entries are brief but show good understanding of concepts. He's especially good at putting definitions in his own words.

Estimate of Grade B

Teacher S. Baker
Subject Social studies

Nate was the technical consultant extraordinaire during our recent hypercard projects on the Civil Rights movement. He had extra help sessions for several classmates during study hall and taught me a few new techniques, too. His project on Medgar Evers was flawlessly researched, with info from a variety of print + electronic sources. He's ready for the electronic age!
Estimate of Grade A-

effort they require. Some parents may be unaware of how many students you're responsible for or how much time it takes to craft a one-page typed narrative. If you communicate to them about what the process requires, they will adjust their expectations accordingly.

2. Create a goals sheet.

Use Figure 6.6 as a template for creating your own goal sheet for students to share with parents. This can be sent home with the letter you write, explaining your evaluation plans. By having students develop goals for the term, and allowing parents the option of commenting on student goals, you will have a starting point later in the term for your written comments.

FIGURE 6.6   A student goal sheet with space for parent comments

Student Name _____ Subject _____

Please bring this goal sheet home and discuss your plans for the term with your parents.

My goals for the term include:

1.

2.

3.

Parent comments:

7 MAKING YOUR OWN RULES

H ave you ever watched a group of neighborhood kids of different ages play an informal game of baseball? Many games begin with the children clustered in a knot, figuring out what the rules will be. The five-year-olds might get four strikes, the ten-year-olds only two. Youngest players get underhand pitches, the oldest get hard fastballs. And the toddlers in the group might be responsible to shag balls. Children have a marvelous innate ability to adjust their rules of play to fit the different developmental stages and temperaments in the group. Before long, everyone is playing together, adjusting the rules as the game progresses.

In this handbook, we've tried to provide you with the rules that have worked for us and for many teachers who write fine report card comments and evaluation narratives. Now that we near the end, it's probably time to tell you that many of these edicts might not apply in your teaching situation. Like the neighborhood baseball games, every admonishment we've given will need to be adjusted and refined according to whom you teach and who you are as a teacher.

A quick look at the myriad of books written about assessment over the last few years reveals a frantic search for the right set of rules to make the task manageable. Portfolio checklists, self-evaluation prompts, new categories for report cards—the mountain of materials published recently reveals teachers' strong needs in the area of writing quality assessments. Maybe we need a radical new notion: teachers will not figure out how to evaluate their students well until they have the courage to find their own way, developing a system uniquely their own.

We hope this handbook has given you a few starting points for thinking about the role of writing in your evaluation system. We hesitate to list examples of narratives as "models" for you to use. Forcing your evaluation needs into someone else's system will exclude too many teachers from the process. Your assessments will need to look different from any we provide as exemplars.

But we also know seeing the final products of other teachers can help you develop your own models. We'd like to close with a few narratives from our own teaching and from the work of colleagues to show how the suggestions we've provided in this handbook may or may not apply as individual teachers write narratives.

Jill Ostrow: Learning Profiles

We begin with one of our favorite writers, Jill Ostrow. Jill is the author of *A Room with a Different View* (1995). She regularly writes "learning profiles" about her multiage (K–3) students' learning. She does not follow our advice of keeping her narratives short. For Jill, the intensity of writing a long and detailed narrative is invaluable for her teaching and for the parents she works with. She explains what she values about writing assessments in a cover letter she sends to parents:

Learning Profile Cover Letter
This folder contains the learning profile for your child for this half of the year. Included is a narrative report commenting on the progress your child is making in class. The narrative is divided into two topic headings: Profile as an independent learner, and profile as a community learner. I have also

included a copy of your child's progress wheel. (I shared these with you at conference time, and you should notice more shaded in now.)

These reports take a very long time to write, yet I am committed to giving parents, as well as future teachers, the most detailed description of the child that I can. I chose to do this type of narrative reporting as opposed to the standard report card four years ago when I came to Wilsonville.

By giving a child a number, the child is compared to other children in the class. I couldn't compare children to one another in a single grade class, let alone a class that spans three grade levels and four age levels. That type of reporting is very much up to the opinion of the teacher. I could give a child a "2," whereas another teacher might give the same child a "3" for something. What does that tell you about the child? I feel that narrative reporting gives information about what each individual child can do. Thus, children are only compared to themselves.

For the last three years I have been writing narratives at Wilsonville and have been asked by all parents to please continue and not do the standard card; so I haven't!

I ask that all parents new to this type of reporting system comment on it, and I have included a sheet for you to jot down your comments for me.

Thanks.

Jill makes her parents full partners in the process of evaluating the learning of their child. She is pretty fearless in sharing her views about the value of different kinds of assessment strategies. The following excerpt is from a four-page learning profile written about Ryan; it includes discussion of his work as a writer and as a math student. We think the narrative reveals as much about what Jill values in her classroom as it does about Ryan's learning:

Learning Profile for: Ryan Bragg
School: Wilsonville Primary
Grades: 1, 2, 3
Teacher: Jill Ostrow
Date: Nov. '94

Days absent: .5

Ryan can construct, create, and express meaning through print exceptionally well. He can write pieces that are so descriptive and detailed that most adults I share them with can't believe they were written by an 8-year-old. His writing has become more refined in that he is beginning to use his talent for description to show the power his words can have; not just "soupy" description for the sake of adding description!

He has totally internalized the concept of leads and his leads have influenced every other writer in this class. One such lead reads:

> The smoke slightly lifted as powder stained
> union soldiers trudged off to the rear. Lieutenant Bragg
> stared grimly at the men screaming and crying for
> help. Black slaves used as grave diggers nudged the
> men laying motionless on the ground.

This is typical of the leads Ryan is able to write. He still favors Civil War pieces, but he has also begun a very funny piece that is totally off-beat and completely different. (It's good to see him "lighten-up" a little bit in his writing!) This piece is about an odd man whose best friend is his cupboard that he has named Bob. A bit different from his intense beautiful Civil War pieces! Here is a little excerpt from this piece:

> Name's Fred. Fred Hooter. Dog's name
> Harry. Harry Hooter. He's dumb. Dumber
> than a box of rocks. Thinks he's cool. Where's
> his chow hat backwards . . . I don't have many
> friends. My best friend is a cupboard. I feed
> him plates and glasses.

Besides being able to use his humor to write different types of writing, he can play with language. The sense of voice in that story is strong. His ability to describe his characters through his writing is phenomenal. Ryan is able to revise and edit anything he writes. He is becoming an excellent editor and realizes that drafting is just one step of the writing process. He knows that revision is vital. He can revise his writing to clarify points he has made or by adding or taking away words or phrases. He can edit his pieces for spelling and to add punctuation he has forgotten in his draft. Ryan knows how important drafting is for him. He knows he can write his ideas quickly to get his ideas out, knowing he will be able to go back over his drafts to refine them.

He is an excellent speller and can use a variety of strategies for spelling and editing unfamiliar words he writes. He can edit misspelled words just by looking at the word and seeing what his mistake was. He can also make a list of possible ways a word can be spelled and choose the one that looks right. He can also look a word up in a dictionary or go to find a place where he has seen that word before. The more Ryan writes, has mini-lessons, and reads, the more conventional spelling he will use when writing difficult words he uses in his drafts.

Ryan can write incredible poetry that is not only filled with description, imagery, and metaphor, but that is extremely thought provoking as well. (Where does he think this stuff up from?) For two poems he wrote this year, he allowed us to use them for a poetry analysis we were doing. Groups of children analyzed poems written by Lucille Crafton, Langston Hughes, and Ryan Bragg! He has been writing longer sentences in his poems as opposed to the single word descriptions he was doing last year. The poems we analyzed were:

Heaven waits for
    the men who perished,
The crackle of rifle
    reminding me of death,
I sit in terror
    face white as snow,
    2 nations
        in a bitter struggle for rights.

When the time comes
    a bullet will
        hiss through me,
I will die now,
    nothing will prove me wrong.
I fear all in war.

(He's how old?)

Ryan can write non-fiction, but for the research project for our study of the Civil War, Ryan has volunteered to be a consultant. He often goes to groups of children who need his help. His name is appearing on many bibliographies!

Ryan has made tremendous progress with his mathematical sense. He is able to use many different strategies to solve problems and never says he can't do something. He will try many solutions and methods to solve a problem.

He can solve specific problems I write as well as very open-ended problems I pose to him. At the beginning of last year, these open-ended problems frustrated him terribly; now he welcomes them. One such problem was for him to describe the number 482. That was all the direction given and he came up with about 5 ways to explain this. He drew pictures showing groups of hundreds, tens, and ones; he wrote, "Well, if you have 400, then add 80, you have 480. Then have 2 more it's 482." He wrote that 482 was an even number, and he wrote the equation: $82 + 400 = 482$. All of these explanations showed me several things. One, Ryan can do open-ended problems like this one and take them as far as he can; two, he has a strong understanding of place value; and three, he can group numbers to write equations on his own.

He can write how he solves equations as well. I asked him to explain in writing or using pictures, how he would solve 21 divided by 3. He wrote, "I put twenty-one cubes into 3 groups and kept giving the groups one. Then there were seven in each group." This type of visual work with manipulatives is very important for Ryan. He is extremely visual but can be missed because he can memorize concepts quickly. What happens is he can memorize a math fact, for instance, but not understand what he did to get the answer. This was the case when he entered the class last year. Now, he can understand and explain what he is doing. When asked to explain his thinking strategy for solving $64 + 38$, he wrote, "Well . . . I knew that $6 + 3$ was 9, so I put that into tens and it was ninety. I added 8 and that's 98 then counted four more and it was 102." The fact that Ryan understands how to group tens like that shows his understanding of addition with large numbers now. He is able to create his own algorithms for doing this. He was taught the conventional algorithm of carrying, but that is not always the most efficient method for him.

He was asked one day to investigate the pattern blocks. He investigated the angles and discovered that if the angle of the square was 90 degrees, that the angle of the long white diamond must be 30 degrees. He did this by putting 3 diamond shapes into the angle of the square. From this discovery, he will be able to figure out the angles of all of the pattern blocks.

He has solved problems using addition, subtraction, multiplication, division, fractions, angles, place value, time, measurement, area, estimation, and complex problem solving. He has written his own complex problems and has had others solve problems he has written . . .

. . . What a respectful, honest, open child he is. He not only is respectful, but he demands respect from others; and when he feels he has been disrespected, he will figure out a way to deal with
it. He is in the process of dealing with one such situation with one adult member in the school who he feels was unjust to him.

What will I ever do without this child in my class? I rely on him, I learn from him, I respect him so much.

There is nothing distant or formal in Jill's words. Her passionate involvement in the learning of her students jumps off the page. She is not afraid to have a strong voice in the writing, including humorous asides to Ryan's parents about his astonishing maturity ("He's how old?"). Her narratives are filled with the breakthrough moments in Ryan's work where his new knowledge, skills, and personality as a learner are revealed. While writing an assessment like this is very time-consuming, we can't help but think that as an adult Ryan will be able to pull this narrative out of a box in the attic, and be transported back to a very special time in his life as a learner.

Terri Austin: Showing Students You Care

Terri Austin teaches at the Chinook Charter School in Fairbanks, Alaska, where she worked with other teachers and community members to develop the school's charter. Terri has long been an advocate of open, thoughtful communication between teachers, students, and parents. Her book, *Changing the View* (1994), demonstrates how students can lead parent conferences.

Terri has two pieces of advice for teachers who want to write narrative assessments: write short narratives if it suits you and don't worry if your narratives are not all the same length. If you write from the heart, using specific examples from the classroom to back up your words, the narratives will be effective. "I try to show the child I care," says Terri. In this narrative written to a student in her K–2 multiage class, Terri demonstrates these principles in action:

Dear Ellie:

Did you know that you remind me of Ramona in the last book we read together? You do because, like Ramona, you are creative, adventurous and full of energy. You do everything with joy and enthusiasm. It's fun to be around you and watch you learn.

In reading, you're into chapter books. I'm glad you are trying them out and finding ones you can read. You've read with a partner and now you are working on the *Case of the Great Train Robbery* with a group of friends. During our discussions you always make thoughtful comments. This tells me you are a careful reader and pay attention to the details as you read. I've also noticed that you read a variety of books, from picture books to chapter books. A good reader reads all different kinds of things.

In writing, you've written a couple of books. When I look at your first piece of writing done at Chinook and what you're doing now, I can see that you are gaining confidence as a writer. You are using more words in your writing and your stories are longer. You seem to know what you want to say when you begin. You've done a lot of writing while at Chinook. You've written letters to a college pen pal, to your parents, and to me. You can now do this easily.

You are zooming along in math. You can add and subtract using Alligator Subtraction and Shake Those Beans. You are able to talk about your homework and how you got your answer. You easily made all sorts of different patterns and you practiced estimation when we guessed the pumpkin's height, weight, and circumference. I've noticed that when you make a math choice, you choose activities that make you think.

Responsibility is an important word at Chinook. We've talked a lot about this word. I see you as a very responsible student. You return your homework on time. You follow directions and you do your job every day. A big part of responsibility is to help others. You do this almost daily. You showed Brett how to tie his shoes. You helped Keisha do the math using the manipulatives. You are usually one of the first to show kindness to someone else.

I would like you to think about your talking. Recently I've had to move you a couple of times because of this. There are so many times when you can talk that when I ask for quiet work you should be able to do this. Think about how you might solve this problem. You are good at solving problems. Let me know what you decide.

You also show how responsible you are during Daily 5 and on our Reflective Fridays. When we do Daily 5, you thoughtfully do each of the five activities. You don't rush, but take your time and complete each one carefully. On Fridays you are able to make a personal plan and then carry it out. This shows that you can set a goal and meet it.

You've learned so much. I can't wait to see what you will learn next.

Love,

Terri

We imagine Ellie can't wait to see what she will learn next, either, because she knows there will be two sets of eyes viewing the changes—hers and her teacher's. Terri builds trust with her students by being

FIGURE 7.1   A letter from Mickey's parents

Dear Mickey,

It's hard to believe how much you've learned in the past 2½ months. You are practically ready to explode into a real "reader." You write all the letters so easily. I remember how the letter "S" was so hard for you— I tried so hard to get you to write it, but after your first week in school you did it perfectly — along with 8, 3 and 5! Mom and Dad are so proud of you. Your interest in math is exciting. Yesterday when you figured out 10 + 10 = 20, you shocked us as well as yourself! You constantly ask about numbers, time and scientific concepts. You are so eager to learn everything. It's exciting to watch your sponge brain soak up so much one day and be thirsty for more the next.

Also, your drawing is incredible. You have such confidence in almost everything you do. I think reflective Friday is helping you to focus on what you want to learn and how to go about it. Also, it's a wonderful way for you to see what you've accomplished during the week—whether it's learning patterns or helping someone in need.

You are a mature responsible boy by nature. Chinook celebrates that and respects your sense of what you want and need to do. Sometimes you need quiet reading time and other times a less studious social interaction. You (we) are very fortunate to be enrolled in a school where the individual's needs come first — daily as well as yearly.

You tell us that running laps outside is your favorite activity, but I think you <u>love</u> the music (you <u>never</u> used to sing) and math the best.

We look forward to seeing your portfolio!

Love,
Mom and Dad

FIGURE 7.2 Mickey's letter to himself

Dear Mickey,

I learned how to write. I practice. I learned how to write cat, dad, mom, and dog. In reading, I learned how to read. I like to read things over and over again to get more practice at it. I've learned how to make big numbers, like on the number line and on the calendar. There are only three more days until Thanksgiving. I know how to do alligator subtraction, geo boards, cuisenaire rods.

I've helped to put books away in the bin. I helped Sean spell. I haven't wrote for him, I just told him the letters. I help clean up. I like to sweep.

I've learned how to be responsible. That was one of my goals. I learned by listening.

I would like to learn how to do subtraction a little bit better.

Love,

specific with them. Her care is evident in the details of her narrative. At Chinook Charter School, parents and students also write letters each term as part of the evaluation. The parent writes to the child, and the student writes to herself. The samples in Figures 7.1 and 7.2 show how everyone at Chinook Charter School is a partner in assessing growth through these written narratives. As these narratives demonstrate, even the youngest learners can discover how to gauge, analyze, and celebrate their learning each term with the support of their parents and teachers.

JEFF WILHELM: AWESOME WITH A CAPITAL "A"

Jeff Wilhelm, author of *Standards in Practice, Grades 6–8* (1996), frequently wrote narrative assessments of his students during his many years as a middle level teacher. He breaks one of the unwritten but pervasive rules that seems to be in place for most teachers writing narratives: teachers feel they must be humorless and measured in their writing. In this narrative written to a student, Jeff's enthusiasm for the student's learning and his sense of fun jump right off the page:

Greetings and Salutations, Sheldon the Great!

I just finished going through your portfolio and it is AWESOME baby, with a capital A! You have caught the fever, my friend! I remember when you couldn't find an implied main idea if it was put on your cafeteria tray right next to the jellied cranberries. And look at you now!

Class Goal: Reading for Main Ideas
First off, as you described in your cover letter, you completely nailed down reading for both directly stated and implied main ideas. I remember at the beginning of the quarter when we were reading *The Voyage of the "Dawn Treader"* and you were having some difficulty figuring out the point of each adventure and how the adventures worked together and created a meaningful sequence. But your last two literary letters from that book (Exhibits C and D in your binder) show that you are understanding the symbolism of Deathwater Island and the main idea or deep meaning that this adventure has for the characters. And I also really liked your explanation of what the dragon story meant to Eustace and how he was transformed by the experience. In that letter you show that you are thinking not just about the point of that episode, but the point of the book so far regarding Eustace's character change. Yeah!

The morals you wrote during our fable sequence show that you can read for central focus. I also loved the series of fables you wrote about the "Greedy Family." The multiple choices of morals you offered after each fable corresponded to the major mistakes readers usually make—too general, too specific, off the point (like totally!) and Right ON! Your group had fun reading those fables too when you shared them in class. (Ever see the Sugar Family or the Nuclear Family on Saturday Night Live? Your fables reminded me of those—I laughed out loud several times.)

Personal Goals: More Organized Writing; Learning
Hypermedia Tools
The examples of issue trees and your web plan for your hyperstack show that you are learning how to classify and chunk information, and how to link

information in ways that are powerful for your reader. Your design diary did a great job of explaining and justifying why you made the links you did and what kind of "work" those links will do for readers. I particularly liked your crosslinks between the mythology cards and the explanations of modern holidays, celebrations and even education!

The interactive quiz in your cultural journalism hyperstack about Norway, and the drag animation on your mythology card show that you learned new things about using hypermedia. I was particularly impressed that these features of your hyperstack were not pure flash, but actually contributed to your point that Norway is a culture that is still very much informed by cultural tales and mores. Your card on traditional foods almost makes me want to eat lutefisk next Christmas—NOT!

Your portfolio was really well organized, too, which I appreciated. The plastic sheaths will keep your entries fresh for posterity and for your biographer, and the color coding helped me find everything.

What can I say? Mr. Friedemann would call you a MAJOR DUDE and he would be right! Thanks for the hard work—this truly displays your learning.

Get this signed by a parent and think a little more about next quarter's goals. I like that you challenged yourself to read more, but what kind of books do you want to read, and for what purposes? Maybe you should set your goal in terms of time instead of pages because it sounds like you might want to read some challenging books.

YERT, DR. W

"YERT" is Jeff's acronym for "Your Excellent Reading Teacher." In this narrative, Jeff manages to highlight many specific strengths of his student, even as he challenges him to think more deeply about his goals for the next quarter. The jokes and asides demonstrate Terri's principle in a different way—Jeff cares enough about his students to provoke their humor and engagement. And then, like Terri, he encourages his student to do more and think harder over the coming weeks.

KELLY CHANDLER: BUILDING ON STUDENT STRENGTHS

For Kelly, the rules about writing narratives include honoring students' responsibility for their work. This includes celebrating what they have done well, but also challenging students to do better. As a high school teacher, her emphasis is on one subject area, with detailed descriptions of growth in reading, writing, and literary analysis. In the following two examples of narratives written to individual high school students, specific areas of strength and need are highlighted. Students know their work is respected enough to be challenged.

Dear Annie,

Your *Sula* paper is one of the finest efforts I've seen from you in two years. It demonstrates some deep thinking and some good use of textual evidence. I especially like your analysis of Sula's name and her return with the robins; both sections are well developed and supported with examples. The paper improved by leaps and bounds as you took it through several drafts. I can see a few places in the paper where the argument needs a little bolstering, some places where you need better transitions, but I'm glad you stopped where you did. Neither of us would have gone through another revision!

I am disappointed that you didn't complete a final draft of your paper on *One Flew Over the Cuckoo's Nest*. I saw some sophisticated ideas about character emerging as you analyzed McMurphy's intentions and his effects on others in the ward. You really needed to refine them more and develop a clearer thesis, though. Remember for this quarter that you need a fair amount of time to take a paper through the brainstorming stage to the final draft. If you don't start early, you won't finish well.

This quarter I would like to see you read some more books with a complicated narrative structure. Both *Sula* and *Cuckoo* demanded more of you as an active reader than most of what you read. I would rather see you read fewer books more slowly, as long as they are challenging. Let's sit down and make a list soon.

Ms. C

Dear Abigail,

Your *Satanic Verses* paper is one of the highlights of the semester for me. It is powerfully, often elegantly, written, and each subsequent revision distilled your ideas into something clearer and more persuasive. In your final draft, you cut the material from the end that muddied the waters of your paper, so to speak—and the work is better for that choice. I especially like your analysis of Rushdie's dual language status and his feminism. Both of these ideas are fresh and interesting; if I remember correctly, your secondary material dealt more with the strictly religious aspects of the text. My only criticism—a minor one—concerns your conclusion, which strikes me as weaker than your introduction—almost a restatement. In general, however, I am proud of you for taking on such a challenge, both with your choice of book and choice of topic.

Your *Piano Lesson* paper is less adventurous than your first, yet still interesting. You balance well the tension that exists within Boy Willie and Berneice. Because they are both complicated people, the viewer/reader cannot simply identify with one over the other. You recognize this and handle it well in your paper. Again, however, your conclusion is the least satisfying part. You cut it a bit short and leave me hanging. And, while I did not want a complete summary of the storyline, your omission of how the situation is resolved seems to be a crucial one. The reader needs to know that Berneice wins out, in a way, and that Boy Willie is transformed in at least a temporary way. He learns a lesson and—I guess—so does she.

I'm looking forward to what you will accomplish in the next quarter. I'd like to see you read some other books from different cultures and deal with some more controversial issues. I would also like to see you write more in-depth, reflective weekly letters on a regular basis, so that you and I can have a dialogue on paper.

Ms. C

By concentrating on only a few instances of reading and response, Kelly works to show she is paying close attention to the habits of her students and to the way their processes are changing. She also encourages both students to collaborate more with her to meet new goals.

Brenda Power: One Small Shard at a Time

Our final narrative, written by Brenda about a teacher she works with, points to changes that will be needed in our profession if there is to be wholesale change in the way students are assessed. Both of us regularly write narrative assessments of preservice teachers and practicing teachers enrolled in graduate programs. We believe the end point for writing narratives, as well as the beginning point for transforming the field, is to change the way teachers themselves are assessed. Until the assessment of teachers becomes more individualized, systematic, and complex, it will be hard for teachers to value writing detailed assessments of their students.

The University of Maine Summer Reading and Writing Program
Narrative Evaluation for David Richardson

Looking for case study artifacts reminds me of a time two summers ago when I searched the North Branch of the Penobscot River for Native American artifacts. I wandered up and down the river bank looking for evidence but for most of the weekend found nothing. Only when I stopped looking for intact pottery and perfect arrowheads did I have my success. Once I had broadened my focus I found a couple of shard pits and left the area with a dozen pieces of evidence that Native Americans had used that site hundreds of years ago. As I wander about our room digging in every corner and as I sift through the journals, I remind myself that evidence accumulates one small shard at a time.

 David Richardson, Journal Entry

 The summer internship for David Richardson has been one of putting many professional pieces together, one small shard at a time. There are numerous professional "selves" he has considered in this work—teacher, learner, student, writer, and leader. This work has been a natural extension of his sabbatic leave this spring. What emerges as the glue that holds all the pieces together is David's reflectiveness. Throughout the internship, David has taken the time to sit back, focus, and consider how individual experiences fit into a larger frame of understanding better and improving his teaching.

 David was usually the first person on site at the internship each morning, long before other teachers arrived. He would read and write, quietly, setting the reflective tone that marked many hours for him at the school. David struggled a bit in the first two weeks of the internship as he tried to define its purpose. While his journal entries in the early days are punctuated with comments showing pleasure in the experience and respect for his colleagues, there is a sense a piece of the puzzle was missing for him. On July 11, he remarks that he has finally realized the true purpose of the internship—to allow colleagues time to reflect on their practice in a community. This is the purpose that emerged for David as most important. He articulates this purpose in another journal entry: "One of my lifelong goals is to learn to be such an observer that every day I learn new things."

 David's daily journal entries aren't written—they are crafted, filled with descriptive language and metaphors that are often dazzling. One of the gifts David should continue to cultivate is his writing ability. His writing has a gentle strength, and he often puts unusual twists into his insights to make them fresh. An example of this is his description of finding something daily to write about in his journal: "Sometimes I need a couple of false starts before I can continue and then my ideas seem to sputter along, hiccuping like a car running on a bad batch of gas. Why? Is it my audience? Is it my habit of waiting for the last moment before looking at the issues of the day?" Because David attends so closely to his own learning processes, he is able to help his colleagues delve more deeply into their own habits and motivations.

David's strength as an observer and colleague were evident in the workshop on "Designing Minilessons" he facilitated with Jenny Smith. The workshop was a masterful mix of taking cues from the needs and experiences of the audience, and presenting new materials to suit the needs of the audience based upon his own experience with minilessons.

As he nears the end of the CAS program, David has much to offer other adults as a mentor and teacher. This is also David's prime time to explore the shards of learning and understanding that are still missing from the "whole" of his understanding of literacy.

Recommendations

1. David should continue to explore his talents and interests as a writer, through books like *poemcrazy* and *Bird By Bird*. David might also apply for the Maine Writing Project (MWP)—he would be an excellent resource for writing teachers in the region. Jeff Wilhelm is director of the MWP.

2. David should consider adjunct teaching for the University of Maine. Good potential courses for him include ERL 537: Literacy Across the Curriculum, and ERL 536: The Writing Process in the Schools. To teach these courses, he might consider "shadowing" another instructor of the course first as part of the process of learning to be an adjunct. If David is interested in adjunct teaching in the future, he should contact Jane Doe, who is responsible for literacy scheduling in 1997–98.

3. The best journal on teaching middle level students is *Voices from the Middle*. This journal also often features articles on poetry, a particular interest of David's. Subscriptions are available by writing the National Council of Teachers of English (NCTE) at 1111 W. Kenyon Road; Urbana, IL 61801.

4. David should consider working with Jenny Smith to develop a small guide for minilesson development. Proposal guidelines for Stenhouse Publishers are attached.

Teachers who receive thoughtful written assessments of their practice and learning can't help but want to write similar narratives for their students. David may or may not follow the advice given in this evaluation. But he has been given some possibilities for continuing to learn and grow. We hope he also has developed some new respect for his strengths as a teacher and learner.

Our wishes for the readers of this handbook are the same as our hopes for David. We hope this book in some small way helps you realize new possibilities for you and your students in writing narrative assessments. It may be a while before your own "big picture" comes into focus and you can figure out how your evaluation system needs to change. Like David, you might need to piece together many small shards of understanding about students, your time, your curriculum, and your writing before you make changes. As you trust your ability to find and break rules in the way you write assessments, we trust you will see your ability and confidence as an evaluator grow.

References

Austin, Terri. 1994. *Changing the View: Student-Led Parent Conferences*. Portsmouth, NH: Heinemann.

Fletcher, Ralph. 1993. *What a Writer Needs*. Portsmouth, NH: Heinemann.

Graves, Donald. 1994. *A Fresh Look at Writing*. Portsmouth, NH: Heinemann.

Irving, John. 1989. *A Prayer for Owen Meany*. New York: Ballantine.

MacLachlan, Patricia. 1985. *Sarah, Plain and Tall*. New York: HarperCollins.

Ohanian, Susan. 1996. *Ask Ms. Class*. York, ME: Stenhouse.

Ostrow, Jill. 1995. *A Room with a Different View: First Through Third Graders Build Community and Create Curriculum*. York, ME: Stenhouse.

Rylant, Cynthia. 1992. *Missing May*. New York: Orchard.

Sadker, Myra, and David Sadker. 1994. *Failing at Fairness: How Schools Shortchange Girls*. New York: Scribner's.

Steinbeck, John. 1937. *Of Mice and Men*. New York: Bantam.

Vygotsky, Lev. 1978. *Mind in Society: The Development of Higher Psychological Processes.* M. Cole, V. John-Steiner, S. Scribner, and E. Souberman, eds. Cambridge, MA: MIT Press.

Wilhelm, Jeff. 1996. *Standards in Practice, Grades 6–8.* Urbana, IL: National Council of Teachers of English.

Annotated Bibliography

Austin, Terri. 1994. *Changing the View: Student-Led Parent Conferences.* Portsmouth, NH: Heinemann. *Discusses Austin's narrative writing process and includes a lengthy sample, as well as lots of examples of students' self-assessments.*

Azwell, Tara, and Elizabeth Schmar, eds. 1995. *Report Card on Report Cards: Alternatives to Consider.* Portsmouth, NH: Heinemann. *Perhaps the best book-length source on reporting to parents. Of special interest are Kathy Egawa and Tara Azwell's "Telling the Story: Narrative Reports" and Richard Driver's "A Math/Science Perspective." Also includes a detailed description of how schools might go about redesigning their report cards.*

Bridges, Lois. 1996. *Assessment: Continuous Learning.* York, ME: Stenhouse. *Many samples of practical assessment tools for the primary grades. Also includes recommendations for other resources on assessment.*

Cambourne, Brian, and Jan Turbill. 1994. *Responsive Evaluation.* Portsmouth, NH: Heinemann. *Shows teachers making first steps toward writing narratives based on observations.*

Drummond, Mary Jane. 1994. *Learning to See: Assessment Through Observation.* York, ME: Stenhouse. Markham, ON: Pembroke. *Provides a strong philosophical basis for moving toward observation and narrative assessment.*

Farr, Roger, and Bruce Tone. 1994. *Portfolio and Performance Assessment: Helping Students Evaluate Their Progress as Readers and Writers.* New York: Harcourt Brace. *Many useful reproducibles of checklists and comment sheets.*

Glazer, Susan Mandel, and Carol Smullen Brown. 1993. *Portfolios and Beyond: Collaborative Assessment in Reading and Writing.* Norwood, MA: Christopher-Gordon. *Chapter 7, "Reporting Progress," describes the process of writing a year-end report and includes a lengthy sample written as a letter to the student.*

Goodman, Ken, Lois Bridges Bird, and Yetta Goodman. 1992. *The Whole Language Catalog: Supplement on Authentic Assessment.* New York: Macmillan/McGraw-Hill. *A comprehensive sourcebook of assessment tools including conference forms, checklists, anecdotal record forms, and more. Also contains sections on self-evaluation for both teachers and students.*

Harp, Bill, ed. 1994. *Assessment and Evaluation for Student-Centered Learning.* 2nd ed. Norwood, MA: Christopher-Gordon. *An edited collection that contains many samples of record-keeping forms, especially in Chapter 10. Also includes an excellent summary of principles underpinning assessment in student-centered classrooms.*

Hewitt, Geof. 1995. *A Portfolio Primer: Teaching, Collecting, and Assessing Student Writing.* Portsmouth, NH: Heinemann. *Includes two complete student portfolios, one by a fourth grader and the other by an eighth grader. Chapter 9 provides a brief but useful discussion of student goal-setting and self-assessment that includes a number of student samples.*

Johnston, Peter. 1997. *Knowing Literacy: Constructive Literacy Evaluation.* York, ME: Stenhouse. *A very comprehensive source on issues surrounding literacy assessment. Chapter 28, "Writing Case Studies," is particularly appropriate for teachers interested in writing lengthy narratives about students' learning.*

Perrone, Vito. 1991. *Expanding Student Assessment.* Alexandria, VA: ASCD. *Includes chapters on assessment in math and science. "Tapping Teachers' Knowledge" by David Carroll and Patricia Carini discusses descriptive review, a collaborative process used by the Prospect School that might help teachers prepare to write narratives.*

Porter, Carol, and Janell Cleland. 1995. *The Portfolio as a Learning Strategy.* Portsmouth, NH: Heinemann. *Of special interest to middle and high school teachers, this book provides nuts-and-bolts information on how to assemble a portfolio, what to include in it, and how to plan next learning steps after the portfolios are completed. Includes numerous student samples.*

Schipper, Beth, and Joanne Rossi. 1997. *Portfolios in the Classroom: Tools for Learning and Instruction.* York, ME: Stenhouse.   *Contains a wealth of helpful information on goal-setting; examples of student, teacher, and parent writing prompts to foster evaluative reflection; and strategies for integrating writing throughout your assessment program.*

Shafer, Susan. 1997. *Writing Effective Report Card Comments.* Jefferson City, MO: Scholastic.   *Aimed at the K–5 teacher, a 64-page guide to writing comments that includes tips and lists of useful phrases. Includes a section with perspectives from four parents on what they're looking for in report card comments. Not as useful for the teacher gearing up to write longer narratives.*

Taylor, Denny. 1993. *From the Child's Point of View.* Portsmouth, NH: Heinemann.   *Very helpful for thinking through the process of writing assessments with other teachers in school settings. Includes about 12 pages of what Taylor calls a descriptive biographical literacy profile.*

Wiener, Roberta B., and Judith H. Cohen. 1997. *Literacy Portfolios: Using Assessment to Guide Instruction.* Upper Saddle River, NJ: Merrill.   *Chapter 9, "Conferencing and Reporting with the Literacy Assessment Portfolio," provides helpful guidelines and sample tools for using conferences as a primary assessment tool, both to gather information for narrative writing and as a way to communicate it to parents and students.*

Woodward, Helen. 1994. *Negotiated Evaluation: Involving Children and Parents in the Process.* Portsmouth, NH: Heinemann.   *Includes separate chapters on how to involve both students and their parents in the information-gathering process. Chapter 6, "Interpreting Evaluation Data," describes how one teacher uses his anecdotal records to develop a narrative.*

Acknowledgments

Jean Smith wrote, "Change is life, growth is optional." We thank the many folks who have helped us adapt and grow in the changing world of written evaluation. There are too many to name, but a few deserve special mention. We thank the teachers who participated in the University of Maine's Summer Literacy Assessment Internship—their work was the inspiration for this volume. Phyllis Brazee has been an important mentor in helping us think through assessment issues. Other literacy colleagues, including Rosemary Bamford, Jan Kristo, Paula Moore, and Jeff Wilhelm, have challenged us to link quality evaluation with quality writing in new ways. Lastly, we thank the numerous fine teachers who allowed us to use the examples and samples of their work that appear in the book.

Philippa Stratton, Martha Drury, and Tom Seavey at Stenhouse provided the usual mix of advice, nudges at deadline, and design savvy that made the process of producing this slim volume a pleasure. Susan Russell's care in attending to the daily administrative details at the University of Maine gives us more time to think and write.

Finally, we thank our families, who patiently endured living rooms overrun with piles of narrative assessments and report cards over the past few months, as we've looked for just the right examples for this book. We promise a less cluttered life (or at least living space!) from now on.